E-Politics, Globalization and Digitalization of Politics

Sinem Eray (ed.)

E-Politics, Globalization and Digitalization of Politics

PETER LANG

Berlin · Bruxelles · Chennai · Lausanne · New York · Oxford

Bibliographic Information published by the Deutsche Nationalbibliothek
The Deutsche Nationalbibliothek lists this publication in the Deutsche Nationalbibliografie;
detailed bibliographic data is available online at http://dnb.d-nb.de.

Library of Congress Control Number: 2025030901

The views expressed in this book are purely that of the author herself and may not in any
circumstances be regarded as stating an official position of Bahçeşehir University.

ISBN 978-3-631-90349-0 (Print)
ISBN 978-3-631-90351-3 (ePDF)
ISBN 978-3-631-94033-4 (ePUB)
DOI 10.3726/b23033

© 2026 Peter Lang Group AG, Lausanne (Switzerland)
Published by Peter Lang GmbH, Berlin (Germany)

info@peterlang.com

www.peterlang.com

Contact for General Product Safety Regulation (GPSR): gpsr@peterlang.com

Table of Contents

List of Figures 7

List of Tables 9

Editor Preface—E-Politics, Globalization and
Digitalization of Politics 11
Sinem Eray

The Digitalization of Political Participation 21
Selcen Altınbaş-Umut

Comparative Analysis of Media Ownership in
Hybrid Regimes: Network Analysis of Authoritarian
Populism in Hungary, Turkey, and Norway 37
Çiğdem Çelik

NATO and "Peace Technology" for Human Security 59
Esra Albayrakoğlu

Classifying New Nationalism: Shifting Perceptions
of Adversaries in Globalized East and West 75
Günce Sabah Eryılmaz

Open Balkan Initiative in the Context of "New Regionalism":
Opportunities, Challenges and Results 99
F. Gamze Çakmak

Prospects for a New Form of E-Democracy: Application of
Blockchain to E-Voting and New Types of Ballot Design 125
Arda Can Kumbaracıbaşı

Bibliography 153

Notes on Contributors 185

Appendix 187

List of Figures

Figure 2.1   Code Map of Political Views and Emotions on the 2024 Local Elections 28

Figure 2.2   Code Distribution for Opinions on Specific Topics 29

Figure 2.3   Code Distribution for Opinions on Social and Social Events 29

Figure 2.4   Code Distribution for General Political Views 30

Figure 2.5   Code Distribution for Emotional Views on the Electoral Process (Positive and Negative Emotions) 30

Figure 2.6   Party Support and Criticism in YouTube Comments on the 2024 Local Elections 31

Figure 2.7   Distribution of YouTube Comments on Election Results 32

Figure 2.8   Distribution of YouTube Comments on Election Process 32

Figure 2.9   Frequency Distributions Related to Media and Information Sources 33

Figure 2.10   Frequency Distributions Related to General Community Reactions 34

Figure 2.11   Frequency Distributions of Opinions on Specific Topics 34

Figure 3.1   Turkey Media Network 2010 187

                 Turkey Media Network 2016 188

                 Turkey Media Network 2022 189

Figure 3.2   Hungary Media Network 2010 190

                 Hungary Media Network 2016 191

                 Hungary Media Network 2022 192

Figure 3.3	Norway Media Network 2010	193
	Norway Media Network 2016	194
	Norway Media Network 2022	195
Figure 3.4	The Size of Largest Two Components 2010–2022	48
Figure 3.5	Number of Components 2010–2022	49
Figure 3.6	Mean Degree 2010–2022	50
Figure 3.7	Eigenvector Centralization 2010–2022	51
Figure 7.1	Application of Blockchain to E-Voting Process	139

List of Tables

Table 2.1   Election Day Media Viewing Rates 27
Table 7.1   Previous Approaches to Utilizing Blockchain Methods 138
Table 7.2   Blockchain in Stages of E-Voting 148
Table 7.3   Hypothetical Types of E-Democracy and E-Voting
            Utilizing AI and Blockchain Systems 152

Editor Preface
E-Politics, Globalization and
Digitalization of Politics

Sinem Eray

Introduction

Globalization, digitalization, new media and new nationalism, as well as new developments in areas such as these, are reorganizing the political, economic and cultural norms of twenty-first century societies. Intercultural interaction, economic integration and technological developments are emerging as a result of globalization. These changes have led societies to transcend their traditional boundaries and strengthen connections between individuals and communities. While globalization facilitates the sharing of cultural and social wealth, it has also created new problems such as economic dependency and identity issues. On the other hand, it deepens social and economic inequalities.

However, digitalization has significantly changed the way people obtain information, communicate, and participate in political processes. Thanks to digital technologies, people all over the world are easily connected and can share information quickly. Especially through social media, individuals' political and cultural interactions are spreading to a wider audience. Apart from its positive aspects, problems such as disinformation, privacy issues, and digital inequality have also emerged as a result of the spread of digitalization. In the digital age, individuals have become more involved in politics, but the impact of these changes on democratic systems and their moral significance are still a matter of debate.

The changes in the media sector have deepened as a result of globalization and digitalization, and with political or economic groups taking control of media organizations, issues such as public access to information and media impartiality have become important topics of discussion. While the control of the media by certain power groups can threaten the openness of democratic processes, ideological and political messages spread through the media directly affect the perceptions and value judgments of societies. Authoritarian and populist discourses spread through the media have been important factors shaping the political preferences and individual identities of societies. At this point, media control has become a critical turning point for the public to understand the democratic structure of society transparently.

The new nationalism movement that emerged as a reaction to globalization and multiculturalism has caused societies to begin to make more distinctions between "us" and "the other." Certain groups have begun to feel the need to protect themselves and emphasize their differences due to globalization, digitalization and the blurring of national identities. This has caused the new nationalist movements that are rapidly spreading in societies to fuel ethnic, cultural and religious divisions. While the new nationalism supports the idea of societies defending their own values on the one hand, it also poses a great threat to global peace and cooperation by deepening social divisions and producing populist discourses on the other.

Transformation and development processes provide new collaborations in interactions between societies. However, on the other hand, they also lead to major changes in the internal politics of nation-states. At this point, the concepts of national borders and sovereignty have begun to change with the new path brought by the global economy and the digital world, and international collaborations have begun to gain more importance. Nation-states that want to adapt to these new conditions are forced to create new policies in domestic politics on security, identity and sovereignty. During the new interaction, all actors need to reorganize their roles both in the international arena and in domestic politics.

These transformations have political consequences that cannot be understood solely through an economic or social lens. New governance models that utilize digital tools in decision-making processes are arising to complement these political institutions that take time to adapt to breakneck technological advances. E-governance blockchain-based voting systems and AI-driven public policy strategies—have all changed the functions of the state in modern political thought. Such developments will have to reassess the democratic nature of representation and accountability, beyond their reliance on bureaucratic structures replaced by digital governance mechanisms.

This book aims to examine the impact of these changes that the contemporary world is facing on societies and how these changes affect international relations. By bringing together views from different disciplines in the context of the challenges and opportunities that emerge in the era of globalization, it will comprehensively address issues such as regionalism, media ownership, digitalization, peace technology, e-democracy and nationalism. While demonstrating the broad impacts of digitalization and globalization on societies, each topic will provide a foundation for understanding today's complex political and cultural structures.

The book will comprehensively discuss many topics, from NATO's peace technology investments to the Open Balkans initiative, from new nationalism theories to media ownership and the impact of digital participation on democratic processes, supported by current examples. In this context, readers will be provided with a valuable resource for understanding the impact of digitalization and globalization on society.

Deepening globalization and digitalization are paving the way for novel political, economic, and cultural dynamics that are fundamentally transforming international relations. Digitalization opens new ways for security, governance, and political participation, but also new forms of threats and challenges—including misinformation, digital authoritarianism, and economic dependence. The changes had influenced not only national governments but also regional collaborations and nationalist movements that had also reacted to globalization, but differently.

Digitalization, Political Participation, and Media Control

Digitalization has increased political participation while also revealing new methods of political participation. The chapter titled "The Digitalization of Political Participation" written by Selcen Altınbaş-Umut examines how political participation has changed using digital platforms during Turkey's 2024 local elections. In her study, Altınbaş-Umut states that user comments made on social media sites such as YouTube are an example of low-cost and superficial participation, which she calls "slacktivism." According to Altınbaş-Umut, although new political participation tools allow people to express their political thoughts, they seem to have little effect on democratic processes. The fact that digital participation does not create a cost on the individual makes it difficult for the individual to maintain a more superficial political stance and develop a broader perspective of political engagement. This study will make a significant contribution to the field by discussing how digital participation methods affect democracy in society and how they direct the political movement of the new generation of young people, especially the Z generation. However, political participation cannot be analyzed in isolation from the role of media. The increasing dominance of media ownership by political elites has played a significant role in shaping public discourse and political preferences.

In the chapter "Comparative Analysis of Media Ownership in Hybrid Regimes: Network Analysis of Authoritarian Populism in Hungary, Turkey, and Norway" written by Çiğdem Çelik; the relationship between media ownership and authoritarian populism provides important information about how the power dynamics between media and politics are shaped in modern societies. As Çelik argues in her study, the control of media outlets by certain political groups in hybrid regimes such as Turkey and Hungary have emerged as the most important tool used by authoritarian-populist governments to consolidate their control over society. We can see that media owners are getting stronger as media organizations start to lose their independence. This process can be seen as the easiest way to easily manipulate public opinion. Çelik stated that media owners have a negative impact especially on authoritarian-populist discourses and that democracy has changed in a negative way. Public opinion is restricted in accessing information by manipulative discourses. Other studies have also clearly detailed that powerful media owners support authoritarian discourses and that even in democratic governments, public access to information is restricted. The potential social consequences of powerful media ownership have become a vital research topic to protect democratic norms. While media ownership remains a critical issue in shaping national political structures, security concerns in the digital age have also gained prominence. The intersection of digitalization and security, particularly in conflict prevention and crisis management, has led to new strategic approaches such as peace technology.

Peace Technology and Human Security

Peace technology offers a new approach to the field of security to improve human security. In this context, Esra Albayrakoğlu, in her study titled "NATO and Human Security through Peace Technology," provides a detailed analysis of NATO's investments in peace technology to increase the security of societies in pre- and post-conflict processes. According to Albayrakoğlu, new technologies have begun to be actively used in many areas such as digital diplomacy, primarily crisis prevention, and then humanitarian aid and post-war rehabilitation. The security of civilians and the protection of human rights are seen as the main objectives of NATO's new strategy for human security. NATO shows us how new peacetech is influencing security strategies. A key part of NATO's peacetech efforts is developing digital and technological solutions to ensure societal resilience in the face of global crises and conflicts. While international security strategies continue to evolve in response to digitalization, the impact of globalization on national politics has also triggered significant reactions. Among these, new nationalist movements have emerged as a strong counterforce to global integration, reshaping domestic and international politics.

The Rise of New Nationalism

Another concept, new nationalism, was born as a reaction against globalization. It has gained strength in the environment of insecurity created by economic and cultural changes in societies. Günce Sabah Eryılmaz's study titled "Classifying New Nationalism: Shifting Perceptions of Adversaries in Globalized East and West" examines the effects of the concept of new nationalism on society in detail. In this study, Eryılmaz emphasizes that new nationalism develops a strong reaction against immigrants and groups seen as "others" by dividing societies into "us" and "them." This study explains that the new wave of nationalism that emerged in Western Europe and the United States is supported by anti-immigrant populist discourses and leads to a separation in society. Unlike traditional nationalism, new nationalism describes how it sees multiculturalism and globalization as a threat and at the same time the efforts it makes while preserving local cultural values. Eryılmaz's study contributes to the literature by comprehensively analyzing how this anti-globalization discourse contributes to the strengthening of nationalist tendencies in various countries. Although nationalism creates internal resistance to globalization, new forms of regional cooperation are simultaneously emerging as alternatives to traditional global economic structures. The Open Balkan initiative serves as an example of such efforts, aiming to strengthen economic and political ties among regional actors.

New Regionalism: The Open Balkan Initiative

Another new phenomenon mentioned in another section is the Open Balkan initiative. Unlike the old regionalism, the new regionalism aims to create a comprehensive cooperation environment by bringing together state and non-state actors. The "Open Balkan" initiative, which was launched especially in the Western Balkans, is seen as an important regional initiative aimed at strengthening the economic, social and diplomatic connections of the countries in the region. In Gamze Çakmak's study titled "Open Balkan Initiative in the Context Of 'New Regionalism': Opportunities, Challenges and Results," the Open Balkan initiative is described as a factor that will allow the Balkan countries to establish a tighter economic and political unity among themselves in line with the European Union membership process. Çakmak says that this initiative emerged to eliminate regional imbalances caused by neoliberal globalization and to accelerate economic growth in the region. The Open Balkan increases regional cooperation by including states, the private sector, civil society organizations and other non-state actors in the process. Other studies also see new regionalism not as a part of globalization but as an alternative to it. The Open Balkans initiative places emphasis on regional cooperation and aims to accelerate the integration of countries in the region into Europe while improving their economic independence. As political structures and regional collaborations evolve, new democratic governance models are also being shaped by digitalization. The rise of e-democracy provides an innovative framework for citizen participation while simultaneously raising concerns about security and inequality.

E-Democracy and the Future of Political Engagement

The chapter titled "E-Democracy" written by Arda Can Kumbaracıbaşı discusses e-democracy theories, the impact of information and communication technologies on democratic life, and the processes by which these new technologies increase social participation. Kumbaracıbaşı states that individuals can play a more active role in areas such as political representation, participation in decision-making processes, and shaping public policies through the internet and digital platforms. E-democracy adds an innovative dimension to traditional democracy models, encouraging direct participation by citizens, increasing transparency, and ensuring accountability of governments. Kumbaracıbaşı emphasizes that despite the potential for digital participation to create inequality, there will also be potential problems such as the security of individuals' personal information, and the security risks this creates.

In summation, the unique combination of digitalization, globalization, nationalism, security and political participation is both altering and reshaping the political context unlike anything before. Digital platforms have reconfigured political participation and discourse as this book shows but they have also opened spaces for media monopolies, fake news, and digital tyranny. Peace technology and regional cooperation initiatives such as the Open Balkan initiative are signs of new global governance opportunities, yet the post-cold war world order based on liberal values is experiencing resistance in the form of new nationalism. E-democracy, while a potential avenue for greater inclusiveness, will face hurdles such as security, digital divide and state control. Both democratization and control trends are complexly interconnected with each other across various fronts like radicalization of social media, surveillance tech, authoritarian narrative shaping, training and tests, alternative sources of information and inquiry, etc. so a multi-dimensional understanding of these transformations and interplay between multiple actors requires integrating virtually all of these new media technologies into all sorts of political conversations. The importance of critical engagement, informed policymaking, and strong democratic institutions will matter more than ever, as societies deal with these changes. By presenting these various perspectives, this book offers a starting point for examining and responding to the various changes we find in politics today.

Conclusion

This book gives an alternate angle by thoroughly exploring the foundations impacting democratic structures and changes prompted to social dynamics in the twenty-first century. New nationalism as social movements and peace technology as an innovative security strategy are important factors affecting societies, especially in the age of globalization, which is rapidly penetrating every aspect of life with digitalization and shaping the media. Every part will offer readers a new interdisciplinary angle with which to dissect the influences of these changes on individuals and societies from diverse points of view. By integrating perspectives from political science, international relations, and media studies, this book provides a broad yet detailed framework for understanding contemporary political transformations. This book will function as a compendium of hallucination to understand the consequences, social and political, of the globalization time.

Digitalization, in turn, has emerged as a double-edged sword for politics. Although this sounds ideal in theory, the rise of digital platforms has not only opened a new era for political participation but has also made us susceptible to algorithmic manipulation, cybercrimes, and digital authoritarianism. As a result of digital media, there no longer exists such a clear-cut delineation between political actors and the citizenry, and grassroots movements as well as individual influencers have been able to influence political discourse in previously unimaginable ways. But meanwhile, these platforms have been used by so many to accomplish the opposite, with the goal of pushing dis-information, changing hearts and minds, and undermining confidence in democratic institutions. The evolving nature of digital participation raises critical questions about the role of media ownership, the influence of polit-ical elites in shaping public discourse, and the extent to which digital tools empower or control societies.

Another major question to work on in this book is what it means for the power structure, both nationally and globally, and what effect globaliza-tion and digitalization are having in that context. Some states use digital governance and transparency tools, while others use the same tools for sur-veillance and control. The increasing centrality of digital infrastructures in governance highlights a crucial dilemma: should digital technologies be regulated to prevent abuse, or should their development remain unre-stricted to promote innovation? This digital freedom will need balancing with regulation, and that delicate balance will define the fate of democracy. E-democracy initiatives, blockchain-voting systems, and AI-assisted gover-nance may increase the efficiency of political processes; however, they also pose ethical and security challenges yet to be resolved. The effectiveness of these digital governance mechanisms will depend on whether democratic principles, such as transparency, inclusivity, and accountability, are prioritized over centralized state control.

Moreover, in the age that is being wired, the spiritual theory of sovereignty is likewise being matured. Challenges to National Sovereignty Cyberspace terrorists, digital warriors, and economic dependencies spawned by techno-logical goliaths do not readily fit into our collective conception of national sovereignty. As cyber warfare, digital espionage, and international data conflicts reshape global power relations, traditional definitions of sovereignty are becoming obsolete. When digital infrastructures are critical for the operationalization of most modern economies, data privacy, digital monopolies or above all, the geopolitical delimitation of the technological race between the West and the East, global political issues are linked to the digital economy. The future of international relations will be shaped not only by military and economic power but also by control over digital networks, artificial intelligence, and data governance frameworks.

In sum, this book analyses political changes that are either driven by globalization and digitalization or possibly (and maybe only temporarily) give rise to some original challenges so that an informed picture balancing possible opportunities and risks can emerge for the theoretical and normative debate in political science. We want to not only point out the difficulties that these changes create but also suggest some potential solutions and policy ideas about how to preserve democratic integrity the more digital we become. In doing so, this book highlights how societies can navigate these transformations by fostering digital literacy, strengthening institutional resilience, and promoting policies that enhance democratic engagement in the digital age.

How societies and policymakers manage these complexities will determine the societal impacts these dynamics have on political participation, governance, and identity. Given the proliferation of unethical digital policies, opaque governance, and the erosion of media pluralism, the need for these principles is more urgent than ever. To safeguard democratic norms, political actors, civil society organizations, and international institutions must collaborate to create adaptive governance models that embrace both innovation and ethical responsibility. This book provides a way of seeing that is intended to help academics, policymakers, or engaged citizens better respond to both the challenges and opportunities of the digital age by looking at many of these issues in a multifaceted manner. By presenting an interdisciplinary perspective, this book serves as both a critical analysis and a guide to navigating the evolving landscape of politics in a digitalized and globalized world.

The Digitalization of Political Participation

Selcen Altınbaş-Umut

ABSTRACT

This study examines the ways in which digitalization is influencing political participation in the context of local elections in Turkey. This study focuses on how YouTube comments reflect the dynamics and impacts of digital political participation. The primary objective of this research is to examine the dynamics and effects of political engagement on digital platforms, with a particular focus on the 2024 local elections, which represent a significant event in Turkish political life due to the debates surrounding the candidates and the potential for significant electoral outcomes. This distinguishes the study from others in the existing literature, thus positioning it to make a valuable contribution to the field. The methodology employed the use of MaxQDA, a qualitative data analysis software, to conduct a thematic analysis of user comments on the most-watched YouTube broadcasts on the day of the 2024 Turkish local elections. Thematic clusters within user comments were assessed, and their implications for digital political participation were evaluated. While the majority of extant studies examine digital participation from a general perspective across social media platforms, this study is distinctive in its focus on YouTube comments, thereby offering an in-depth examination of users' reactions to the electoral process. By utilizing the 2024 local elections in Turkey as a case study, this research enhances its contribution to contemporary scholarship on digital political participation.

Keywords: Political Participation, Digital Political Participation, 2024 Local Elections

Introduction

Political participation can be defined as the actions undertaken by individuals with the intention of influencing governmental and political processes. In his seminal work, Political Participation, L. Milbrath (1965), a pioneering figure in the field of political participation, proposed a three-category typology. This included spectator activities, transitional activities, and gladiatorial activities. This classification is based on the degree of intensity and difficulty associated with the actions in question. In accordance with Milbrath's conceptualization, activities of a relatively low intensity, such as displaying a party badge or expressing an opinion on a political issue, are classified as "spectator activities." In contrast, more demanding actions, such as attending political meetings or establishing a relationship with a political leader, are classified as "transitional activities." The most intense and challenging actions, such as assuming an active role in political campaigns, attending strategy meetings, or running for office, are categorized as "gladiatorial activities" (Dursun, 2018, p. 104).

The concept of "spectator activities," as defined by Milbrath, can be seen to have parallels with the rise of digital activism in the context of today's increasingly digitalized world. These activities, which provide minimal participation in political processes, align with Morozov's concept of "slacktivism," which describes the low-effort, low-risk nature of contemporary digital political participation. The act of commenting, liking, or sharing political content on social media platforms can be considered an example of slacktivism. Morozov posits that slacktivism encourages individuals to engage in these symbolic, low-effort activities rather than more intensive "gladiatorial" political actions (Morozov, 2011).

This study examines the evolving dynamics of political participation in the context of digitalization, with a particular focus on the manifestations of these dynamics in the context of local elections. The analysis is informed by the theoretical frameworks of Milbrath's typology of political participation, particularly the concept of "spectator activities," and Morozov's conceptualization of slacktivism, which addresses the phenomenon of digital activism. The advent of digital platforms has led to an expansion and reshaping of low-intensity, risk-free forms of participation, the majority of which fall under the category of "spectator activities." In particular, an examination of users' reactions to electoral processes via YouTube comments provides insights into the evolution of political participation through digitalization. The principal aim of this study is to examine the dynamics and consequences of digital political participation and to identify the ways in which platforms such as YouTube influence political processes. Thematic analysis is employed to examine user comments posted under the most-watched programs broadcast on YouTube during the 2024 local elections, which constituted a pivotal event in Turkish political life. This analysis demonstrates how these comments exemplify digital political participation. The study begins with a conceptual overview of political participation and its digitalized forms, followed by a literature review. It then presents the analysis, findings, and conclusion.

Conceptual Background: Digitalizing Political Participation

Political participation encompasses the various ways in which individuals engage with political processes, and these processes can be classified in multiple ways. Lester W. Milbrath's classification provides a framework for understanding traditional forms of political participation, emphasizing the intensity and modalities of individual involvement. However, with the advent of digitalization, political participation has extended beyond these traditional categories, evolving into new and dynamic forms. Digital political participation has the potential to redefine Milbrath's spectrum by introducing novel ways of engagement. In this context, digital political participation refers to individuals participating in political processes via the internet and digital media tools, fundamentally altering the nature of political engagement by transcending time and spatial boundaries. Digital platforms, particularly social media, have emerged as the new face of political participation, offering unique opportunities for political expression and engagement.

Digital political participation, which refers to citizens' involvement in democratic processes through digital media and internet-based tools, has become increasingly significant in modern politics. This form of participation offers individuals a platform to express their political opinions and take action via tools such as online campaigns, e-petitions, blogs, and social media platforms (Dahlgren, 2013). Theocharis and van Deth (2018) define digital political participation as a broad concept encompassing all forms of political actions facilitated by digital technologies. These digital forms of participation are often complementary to traditional political participation methods but offer less formalized and institutionalized structures. Digital political participation facilitates political mobilization and engages individuals in political processes. Loader, Vromen, and Xenos (2014) emphasize that social media has emerged as the most prominent form of digital political participation, particularly among young people. Unlike traditional hierarchical structures, the horizontal nature of social media platforms allows young people to organize and disseminate their political views more rapidly. These platforms make political participation more accessible and expedite mobilization processes. These studies are aligned with Morozov's (2011) critique of slacktivism. Morozov contends that while digital environments provide low-cost, easily accessible forms of participation, they often result in superficial engagement. Actions such as signing online petitions or liking posts, while perceived as political participation, frequently lack the capacity to effect substantial real-world change.

One of the most notable characteristics of digital political participation is its low cost and wide accessibility, which draws larger audiences into political engagement (Dahlgren, 2013). Combined with its minimal risk, digital activism has gained increasing significance. However, this form of participation also carries the inherent risk of remaining superficial, as the depth and impact of such engagement continue to be debated. The growing prominence of this concept has prompted its emergence as a central focus in various studies within the literature.

Digitalized Political Participation Through Social Media in the Literature

Digital political participation, particularly through social media and digital platforms, has begun to reshape how citizens engage with political processes. This transformation allows digital media tools to involve individuals in these processes in unprecedented ways. Studies reveal that digital platforms are not merely for information sharing but have also become significant spaces for political participation and digital activism. Consequently, many academic studies have explored this phenomenon.

Chen and Wang (2022), for example, investigated the effects of YouTube comments on online political behavior, highlighting the platform's role in misinformation and online aggression. Their study underscores YouTube's potential as a space where individuals actively participate in political debates, beyond just accessing or disseminating information. Similarly, Thelwall (2018), focusing on social media data analysis, explored how user comments on digital platforms, especially those with political content, contribute to qualitative data analysis. Kalogeropoulos et al. (2017) examined the demographic and socio-economic traits of users who comment on online news shared on social media platforms. Their research emphasized that social media participation can foster echo chambers, which in turn intensify political polarization. They argued that increased political debate on social media could reinforce existing views, limiting exposure to alternative perspectives. Öztürk and Zeybek (2020) analyzed the role of

YouTube in political campaigns during the 2019 Istanbul local elections, demonstrating how this platform has become a powerful tool for direct voter interaction. The rise of YouTube as a medium for digital political participation illustrates its growing influence, particularly among young voters. Çağlak and Pekcan (2022) discussed Babala TV's impact on young audiences, asserting that digital platforms offer new arenas for political views to be shared and debated. Likewise, Özmen (2022) studied the interaction between social movements and political parties in the digital age, highlighting how the digital ecosystem has transformed political participation. This study posits that digital technologies serve as more than communication tools for political parties; they have also given rise to new forms of political organizations, such as "digital parties," which operate beyond traditional structures and offer new forms of direct and active participation. Lastly, Güngör (2017) discussed how information and communication technologies are influencing political participation, arguing that digitalization might shift representative democracy toward more direct democracy. While digital platforms have made political participation more accessible, they have also opened new channels for political deliberation, transparency, and oversight of public governance.

Numerous studies on digital political participation, like those mentioned, occupy a prominent place in the literature. Given the focus of this study, the literature reviewed is primarily limited to works that explore digital political participation through social media. While existing studies often examine political participation across various social media platforms, this study uniquely concentrates on digitalized audience activities through YouTube comments. By doing so, it analyses users' reactions to electoral processes within a more focused framework. In this regard, the study offers a significant contribution to the literature by providing a deeper understanding of how digital platforms influence democratic participation.

Digitalization of Political Participation: The Case of 2024 Turkish Local Elections on YouTube

Methodology

To explore the dynamics of digital political participation on YouTube, this study analyses the comments from the most-watched broadcasts during the 2024 Turkish local elections. In this context, user comments on various news programs posted on YouTube are considered as expressions of digital political participation. The thematic analysis of YouTube comments was conducted using the qualitative data analysis software MaxQDA. YouTube, with its video-based and more in-depth content, allows users to leave longer and more reflective comments. This feature distinguishes YouTube from other platforms. In contrast, platforms such as Twitter and Facebook are characterized by quicker, more spontaneous reactions, where participation is often limited to short-term, instantaneous interactions. Thus, YouTube comments were chosen for analysis in this study.

In the data analysis, a thematic coding method was used to examine how YouTube user comments reflect digital political participation. The coding process, conducted through MaxQDA software, was structured into main themes and sub-themes. The main codes were organized around general political themes, emotional reactions, opinions on social and societal events, and specific topics related to the election process. Under the "General Political Themes" category, codes such as "Reactions to Election Results" (positive, negative, neutral), "Party Support and Criticism" (comments on specific parties or candidates), and "Election Process" (evaluations on the fairness of the elections) were developed. These codes allowed for a detailed analysis of users' reactions to election results and political actors. The "Emotional Themes" category analyzed the emotional expressions conveyed by users in their comments. Comments were categorized into three sub-themes: "Positive Emotions" (happiness, hope), "Negative Emotions" (anger, disappointment), and "Neutral or Ambiguous Emotions." Additionally, expectations for the future were coded as a separate category. Under the "Social and Societal Themes," the reactions of the public to the election process were analyzed. The "Social Reactions" code captured opinions on social dynamics such as polarization and unity, while the "Media and Information Sources" code addressed comments on the role and reliability of the media during the election. Finally, under "Specific Issues," comments on key political topics such as the economy, education, healthcare, and foreign policy were coded. Notably, the economic situation emerged as a significant factor influencing users' reactions to the election results, and it was analyzed in detail within this theme.

The dataset includes the following videos, which were broadcast on election day and reached a broad audience:

Table 2.1. Election Day Media Viewing Rates

Election Special Broadcast (Teketek)	4.9M Views
Local Election Broadcast (Sözcü)	3.4M Imaging
2024 Local Elections Special Broadcast (Cüneyt Özdemir)	2.1M Imaging
Istanbul Election Results (Sözcü)	1.1M Imaging
Local Election 2024 Special Broadcast (Halk TV)	1M Imaging
Turkey at the Ballot Box Broadcast (Habertürk)	698K Views
2024 Local Election Broadcast (Sözcü)	694K Views
2024 Live Election Results Stream (Haberglobal)	692K Views
2024 Local Elections Special Broadcast (Habertürk)	659K Views

In the process of analyzing the comments, the code map and code matrix browser functions were utilized to examine the distribution of comments and to identify prominent themes. Through the creation of specific themes and codes, various aspects such as users' political tendencies, emotional reactions, party support, and criticism were analyzed. Political events and themes that were frequently mentioned during the analysis were tagged with thematic codes based on the content of the comments, and the relationships between these codes were further explored. Additionally, emotional reactions to the election process and comments on social events were evaluated within this framework.

Findings

The initial step involves the presentation of the codes that are most frequently mentioned in conjunction with one another. This is illustrated in Figure 2.1, which has been generated through the utilization of the code map function. The map illustrates the interconnections between codes and the frequency with which they are mentioned in conjunction with one another. The width of the lines is proportional to the frequency of mention of the codes in question. In addition, users of YouTube who referenced the code "positive" also mentioned the codes "happiness," "support for CHP," "hope," and "criticism of AKP." Additionally, users who referenced the negative code also mentioned criticism of the CHP, feelings of anger, disappointment, worry, and support for the AKP. The code "positive" was one of the most prominent and frequently mentioned during the electoral process. This category is closely associated with the themes of support for the CHP, happiness, and hope. This indicates that positive feedback regarding the election results is directly correlated with support for the CHP. Negative comments are strongly associated with criticism of the AKP. Negative emotions, including concern, anger, and disappointment, are associated with these criticisms. This indicates that the criticism of the AKP during the electoral process was accompanied by pronounced emotional responses. Specific topics, including economic crisis and migration and refugee policies, were found to be associated with comments on the election results and parties. The economic crisis emerges as a prominent theme, both in terms of its perceived impact on electoral outcomes and its frequent prominence in political discourse.

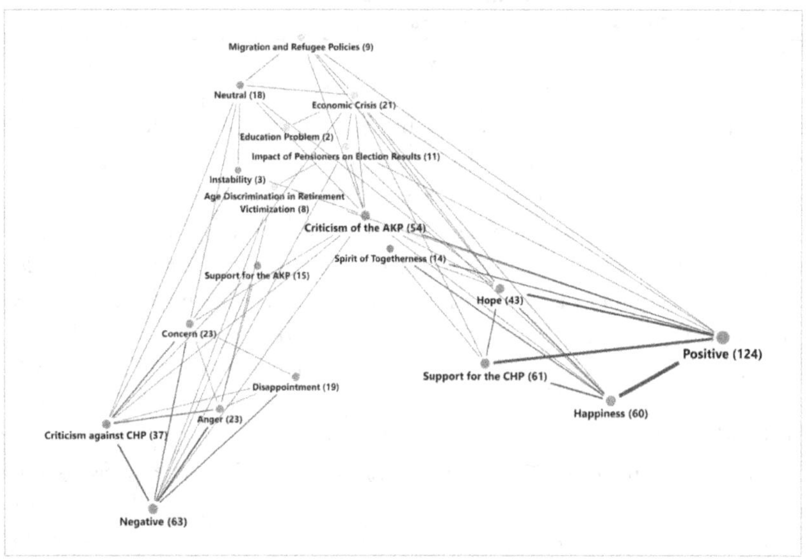

Figure 2.1. Code Map of Political Views and Emotions on the 2024 Local Elections

The results of the analysis conducted with the code matrix scanner indicate that the code "Economic Crisis" had the highest frequency and was frequently mentioned, particularly in the "Teketek" and "Cüneyt Özdemir" broadcasts. The economic crisis emerges as a pivotal theme influencing the electoral outcomes. The code pertaining to the impact of pensioners on election results was especially prominent in the "Haber Global" and "Cüneyt Özdemir" broadcasts. The influence of the elderly on electoral outcomes was a recurring topic of discussion. The theme of migration and refugee policies was a prominent feature of the "Teketek" and "Cüneyt Özdemir" broadcasts. This indicates that the topic of migration and refugee policies constituted a significant element of the electoral discourse. Figure 2.2 offers a visual representation of this data.

Code System	Habertürk 1	Haber Global	Sözcü 1	Habertürk 2	Halk Tv	Sözcü 2	Cüneyt Özdemir	Sözcü 3	Teketek	SUM
OPINIONS ON SPECIFIC TOPICS										0
Impact of Pensioners on Election Results										11
Migration and Refugee Policies										9
Education Problem										2
Age Discrimination in Retirement Victimization										8
Economic Crisis										21
Σ SUM	5	13	0	0	2	4	6		14	51

Figure 2.2. Code Distribution for Opinions on Specific Topics

The "Haber Global" broadcast exhibits the highest frequency of instances of biased media coverage. This indicates that the matter of media impartiality was a recurring topic of debate throughout the electoral process. The Spirit of Togetherness code is observed with notable frequency, particularly in the "Teketek" and "Sözcü" broadcasts. This indicates that the cohesion of society was a significant topic during the electoral process, and that a constructive perspective was evident in the commentary on social events. (See Figure 2.3)

Code System	Habertürk 1	Haber Global	Sözcü 1	Habertürk 2	Halk Tv	Sözcü 2	Cüneyt Özdemir	Sözcü 3	Teketek	SUM
OPINIONS ON SOCIAL AND SOCIAL EVENTS										0
Media and Information Sources										0
Biased Media										19
Having Impartial Media										5
General Community Reactions										0
Spirit of Togetherness										14
Σ SUM	3	8	4	3	2	1	1	1	15	38

Figure 2.3. Code Distribution for Opinions on Social and Social Events

Upon analysis of the code pertaining to general political views, it became evident that the code "Positive Comments on Election Results" was a prominent feature, particularly in the "Sözcü" and "Teketek" broadcasts. This indicates that most individuals expressed positive sentiments in response to the election results. In contrast, negative commentary on the election results was predominantly concentrated in the "Sözcü" and "Haber Global" broadcasts, reflecting a prevailing sentiment of discontent with the electoral outcome. The codes indicating criticism of the AKP and support for the CHP were observed with high frequencies in the "Sözcü" and "Teketek" broadcasts. As illustrated in Figure 2.4, these findings indicate that attitudes toward the parties were largely discernible during the electoral process.

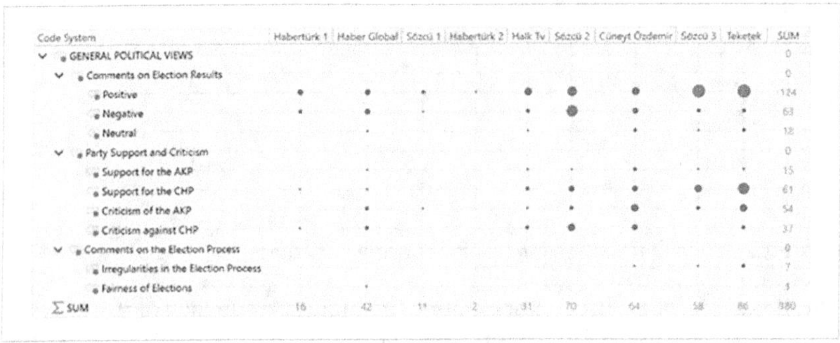

Figure 2.4. Code Distribution for General Political Views

Ultimately, the emotional reflections of the election process revealed a notable prevalence of positive emotions, such as hope and happiness, within the "Sözcü" and "Teketek" broadcasts. This indicates that the election results were a source of hope and happiness for a significant proportion of the population. The negative emotions of concern and anger were particularly prevalent in the "Sözcü" and "Halk TV" broadcasts. This indicates that the election process also evoked feelings of anxiety and anger. (Figure 2.5).

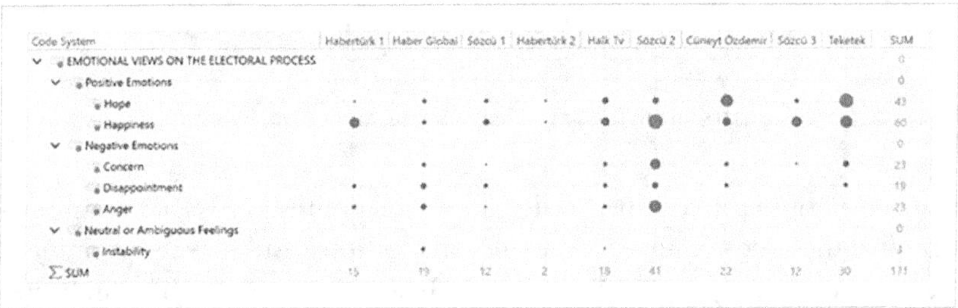

Figure 2.5. Code Distribution for Emotional Views on the Electoral Process (Positive and Negative Emotions)

Considering these findings, it is evident that comments on digital platforms serve as a clear reflection of the public's reactions to the electoral process and their level of support for the various political parties. Furthermore, issues such as the economic crisis and media impartiality are of central importance in the context of election debates.

Upon examination of the frequency distributions pertaining to party support and criticism, it becomes evident that the sub-codes within the analyses warrant particular attention.

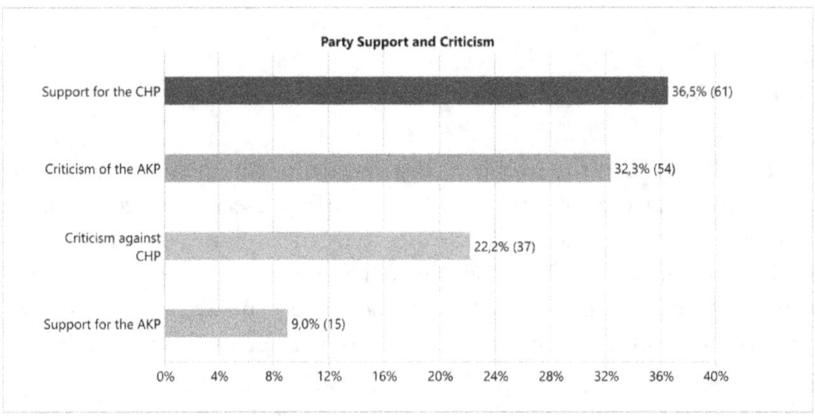

Figure 2.6. Party Support and Criticism in YouTube Comments on the 2024 Local Elections

As illustrated in Figure 2.6, the frequency distribution indicates that 36.5% of YouTube users expressed support for CHP. This support was particularly evident in the context of Ekrem İmamoğlu's electoral success. Users articulated their aspirations for İmamoğlu's future achievements and asserted that they view him as a prospective leader of Turkey. Furthermore, 32.3% of users articulated their disapproval of the AKP and articulated discomfort with the economic issues and immigration policies. In contrast, criticism of the CHP constituted a significant proportion of user feedback, accounting for 22.2% of the total. In these critiques, the CHP was particularly criticized for its lack of services and its performance in local governments.

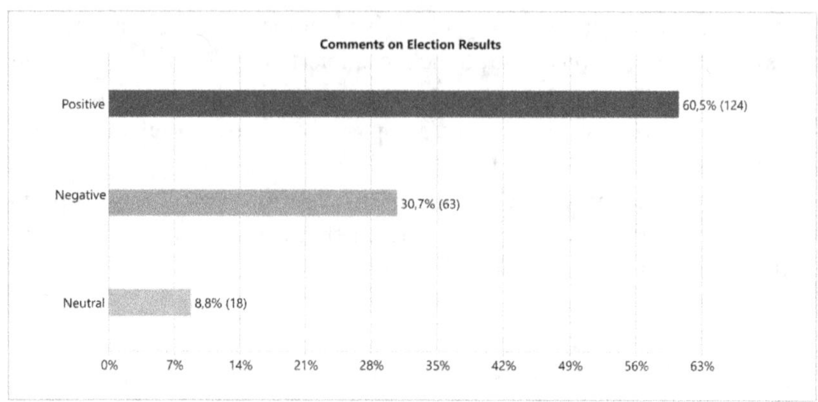

Figure 2.7. Distribution of YouTube Comments on Election Results

Figure 2.7 illustrates the frequency distribution of comments pertaining to the electoral outcome. A total of 60.5% of YouTube users expressed a positive reaction to the election results. These users typically expressed joy at the success of the CHP and Ekrem İmamoğlu, as well as optimistic expectations for the future of Turkey. A total of 30.7% of respondents expressed discontent with the election results, offering negative reactions. These users offered critiques of the election result, particularly about AKP policies. A further 8.8% of users adopted a neutral stance in their response to the election result.

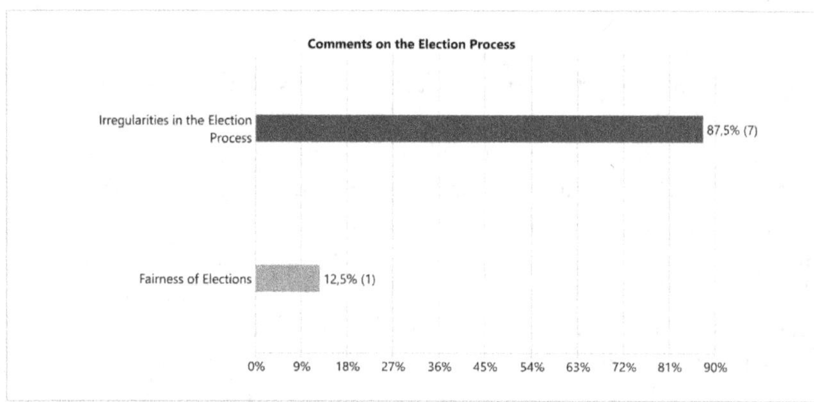

Figure 2.8. Distribution of YouTube Comments on Election Process

Regarding commentary on the electoral process, 87.5% of YouTube users asserted the existence of irregularities. These users asserted that certain regions were subject to electoral fraud, that there were discrepancies in the tallying of invalid ballots, and that there were grounds for suspicion regarding the registration of voters. A total of 12.5% of respondents indicated that the electoral process was conducted in a fair and orderly manner, with no discernible irregularities. (Figure 2.8)

Figure 2.9 illustrates that 79.2% of YouTube users expressed discontent with the perceived bias of media channels during the electoral process, while 20.8% endorsed the value of impartial media. Notable comments included criticism of media channels for distorting the results or disseminating misinformation, as well as praise for the significance of impartial reporting. Users offered particularly scathing criticism of certain channels' purportedly biased coverage and attempts to manipulate the election results.

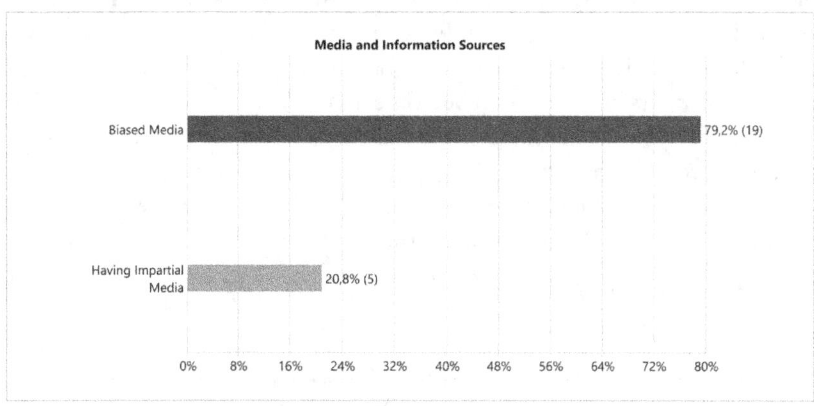

Figure 2.9. Frequency Distributions Related to Media and Information Sources

An examination of the public reactions (Figure 2.10) reveals that the unity spirit of the society during the election process was a prominent feature. All YouTube users (100%) attested that the society exhibited a spirit of unity and voted in favor of democracy and brotherhood in the local elections. Voters in the eastern and south-eastern regions demonstrated this spirit and underscored the significance of unity for Turkey's future. The comments indicate that unity is a critical factor for Turkey to overcome the challenges it currently faces.

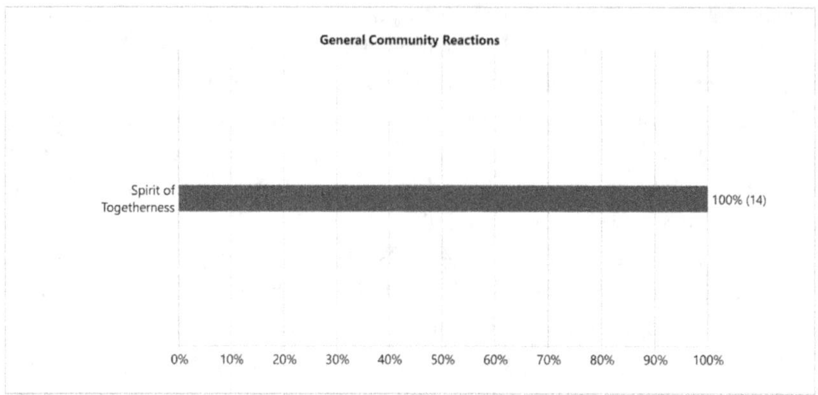

Figure 2.10. Frequency Distributions Related to General Community Reactions

Figure 2.11 presents the opinions of YouTube users on specific issues. Of the respondents, 41.2% indicated that the economic crisis influenced the outcome of the 2024 local elections. Twenty-one-point six percent of users identified the role of pensioners in the election outcome. Furthermore, criticism of specific issues was notable, including refugee policies (17.6%) and the victimization of those at retirement age (15.7%).

Economic difficulties, low remuneration, and inadequate pensions were frequently mentioned. Furthermore, the comments indicated that pensioners played a pivotal role in the election, as evidenced by the "revenge of

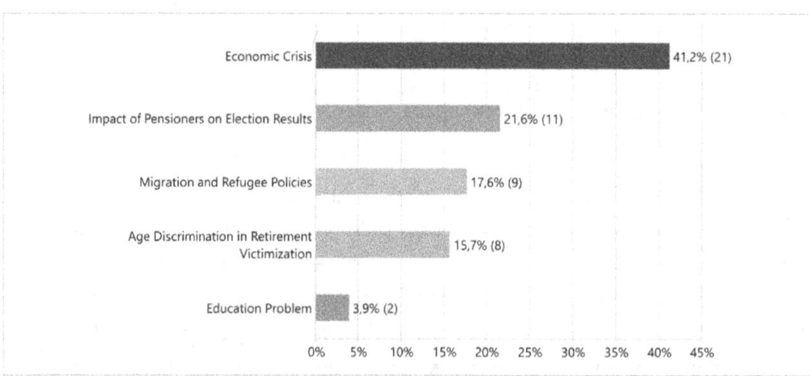

Figure 2.11. Frequency Distributions of Opinions on Specific Topics

Comparative Analysis of Media Ownership in Hybrid Regimes: Network Analysis of Authoritarian Populism in Hungary, Turkey, And Norway

Çiğdem Çelik

ABSTRACT

This study examines the relationship between media ownership and the distribution of information in Hungary and Turkey, which have differing levels of authoritarian populism, as well as in democratic Norway, from 2010 to 2024. This research uses network analysis and the regime classification framework to examine the influence of media ownership concentration on the dissemination of political narratives and public discourse. The study's findings reveal a stark contrast in media ownership patterns, with Hungary and Turkey exhibiting higher levels of ownership concentration, which aligns closely with political elites and supports the propagation of authoritarian-populist agendas. On the other hand, Norway demonstrates a more decentralized media landscape, which supports a broader and more balanced information flow. This study highlights the significant impact of media ownership concentration on changing political discourse and facilitating the dissemination of authoritarian populism. It demonstrates that authoritarian-populist actors exploit the current ownership arrangements of the news media and aggressively interfere in ownership relationships to increase their control over the dissemination of information.

Keywords: Media, Hungary, Turkey, Authoritarianism, Populism

Introduction

Actors in authoritarian and hybrid regimes, whether they are from the government or not, have become skilled at using digital technology to control the flow of information for their own benefit. This includes not only restricting freedom of expression but also monitoring, regulating, and exerting control over the people. In today's digital age, the control and manipulation of information have become powerful tools for actors in authoritarian and hybrid regimes (Aydın-Düzgit, 2020). Media ownership concentration is one of the key methods they use to influence storytelling and manage public perception. The key factors that contribute to the concentration of media ownership and its impact on the spread of authoritarian-populist narratives include political power, economic interests, and the manipulation of media regulations (Gilens & Hertzman, 2000).

Numerous studies examining the link between media and populism have highlighted the significant connection between conservative media platforms and the creation of echo chambers that foster right-wing populism (Jamieson et al., 2010). Additionally, several studies have highlighted the significance of politically motivated media ownership in bolstering populism in certain countries (Esser et al., 2017). These studies suggest that media ownership concentration plays a crucial role in shaping political discourse and promoting authoritarian populism. Many studies have also shown that the privatization of media markets plays an important role in providing media support to authoritarian populists, especially in hybrid regimes (Doroshenko, 2018). Moreover, Baker (2006) emphasizes the relationship between the rise of authoritarianism and the erosion of the "principle of democratic property distribution" (Baker, 2006). As a result, media outlet ownership and control are major concerns.

Authoritarian information control is not a new phenomenon, but the modern methods used for this objective are original (Freedman, 2021). The digital authoritarian toolbox in 2023 includes a wide range of technologies, including social networking websites, artificial intelligence, spyware, video surveillance systems, and traditional mass media ("Unfreedom Monitor Global Voices," 2023). Global observations show a rapid integration of these technologies and the enactment of laws and rules that shape information systems and govern communication. This results in a substantial erosion of essential liberties and human rights, as well as the rights of individuals in both the virtual and real worlds. In hybrid regimes, the concentration of these new tools and methods in certain hands is an effective yet often overlooked strategy (Bátorfy & Urbán, 2020; Wigell, 2019). Therefore, it is crucial to continue researching and understanding the relationship between media ownership concentration and the spread of authoritarian populism (Bardi et al., 2014).

This study distinguishes itself from other studies that adopt a populist approach by focusing on media ownership as a major aspect of authoritarian populism and hybrid regimes, rather than relying solely on cultural and discursive models. This research recognizes that populism can manifest as a sort of "performance," "style," or "rhetoric" (Benvenuto et al., 2012; Laclau, 2005; Moffitt & Tormey, 2014) that emphasizes the divide between "the people" and "the elites" (Mudde, 2004). Yet, it also seeks to emphasize the concrete and institutional dimensions of populist politics. Authoritarian-populist governments under hybrid regimes maintain stability by garnering support and co-opting a wide range of the national capitalist elite (Bugaric, 2019; Svolik, 2012). Authoritarian-populist governments in hybrid regimes often assist and support associated businesses to operate in local markets under favorable conditions (Esen & Gumuscu, 2018). Authoritarian populism often involves a dislike for diversity, and its proponents strategically manipulate ownership structures to diminish economic diversity (Chesterley & Roberti, 2018).

Media ownership refers to the control over print, broadcast, and digital news outlets that disseminate information to the public. Concentrated ownership by a small number of individuals or entities can impact which news stories are distributed and how they are presented (A. Bennett, 2023; Van Der Wurff, 2008; Vizcarrondo, 2013; Winseck, 2008). This concentration of ownership can lead to biased reporting, limited perspectives, and the promotion of narratives that align with the interests of those in power about leaders and issues (Hellmann, 2021). For instance, if all the reports concerning leaders are favorable, individuals may be inclined to offer their support, despite any existing issues. As such, it is necessary to examine the influence of media ownership on public opinion and democratic processes (Bardi et al., 2014). Moreover, understanding the role of media ownership in the spread of authoritarian populism and hybrid regimes is crucial for identifying potential threats to democracy and developing strategies to counteract them. Studying media ownership in different political systems is essential for gaining insight into how the concentration of media control can impact the dissemination of information. This influence may potentially bolster authoritarian rulers by restricting diverse perspectives and managing public discourse (Aguiar, 2017). By analyzing how media ownership is utilized in various political environments, we can gain insight into the methods employed by authoritarian populists to influence public perception and sustain authority. This underscores the significance of a diverse media landscape for upholding democratic governance.

This framework seeks to investigate the influence of media ownership concentration on the spread of political narratives and public discourse in various political systems. In particular, the study will focus on authoritarian populism in Hungary and Turkey compared to democratic Norway between 2010 and 2024. In Hungary and Turkey, the concentration of media ownership in close relations with political elites has facilitated the spread of authoritarian-populist agendas. However, Norway stands out with a decentralized media landscape and a balanced and diverse public discourse. This study aims to focus on the impact of media ownership concentration on the spread of authoritarian-populist discourse and its implications for public debate. The study also delves into the investigation of media ownership concentration in various regime types, specifically examining this relationship in Hungary, Turkey, and Norway, all of which have distinct political regimes.

A Theoretical Approach to Media Ownership Concentration and Authoritarian Populism

Theories concerning regime types, particularly authoritarian populism and the concentration of media ownership, uncover the intricate dynamics influencing modern political environments (Bennett, 2023). Many studies in this context suggest that the nature of political regimes influences media ownership concentration. Democracies generally exhibit higher media freedom compared to autocracies, which often have a more concentrated and controlled media landscape. Scholars in the field of critical political economy of communication examine the ownership and management of the media to understand how it affects the variety of media owners and the media's role in public life and political discussions (Baker, 2006; Hanretty, 2014). When there is an excessive concentration of media ownership, it inevitably leads to a decline in democratic safeguards. This includes the weakening of the media's role as a "watchdog," which serves to prevent abuses of economic or political power and can result in biased reporting and a limited diversity of viewpoints (Baker, 2006; B. Birkinbine et al., 2016). Concentrated media ownership has implications not only for the pluralism of media content, but also for a country's democratic state. The "democratic distribution principle" implies a wide dispersal of power in public discourse and suggests that democracy requires a maximum dispersal of media ownership (Baker, 2006; Hamilton, 2007; Josifides, 1997). The rise of authoritarian populism, characterized by a division of society into "us" versus "them," often results in hybrid regimes that combine democratic and authoritarian elements, as seen in Hungary, Poland, and Turkey (Fuchs, 2018; Hughes & Vorobyeva, 2021; Wigell, 2008). In competitive authoritarian regimes, media ownership concentration often mirrors the views of powerful elites, stifling media independence and contributing to regime stability, as seen in Ukraine (Stier, 2015).

A larger quantity of media outlets does not necessarily ensure media diversity, as Murdock (1983) points out. When participation in media markets lacks variety, it leads to a controlled information environment known as "echo chambers" (T. Bennett, 1983). This is why numerous scholars in the field of communication contend that in markets with high concentration, powerful media owners can circumvent democratic oversight mechanisms and emerge as significant political players capable of shaping election results and regulatory measures (Karadimitriou et al., 2022; Meier & Trappel, 2007). Concentrated media ownership thus carries a significant risk of corrupting politics by serving the interests of both media and political actors (Karadimitriou et al., 2022; Tomaz & Trappel, 2022). Baker's (2007) and Freedman's (2018) evaluation of the control of media ownership in relation to the rise of authoritarianism and populism is extremely pertinent. According to Baker (2006), media ownership is quite striking, and high media concentration benefits populists in two ways. First, populist leaders gain more visibility, and the promotion of pro-government populist messages leads to increased advertising revenue and other commercial benefits (Baker, 2006). Second, the higher the level of media ownership concentration, the more extensive and influential populist content becomes (Baker, 2006). According to Freedman (2018: 611), the number of media outlets is significant, particularly in competitive media environments where there is intense competition for attention. This contest fosters compelling reasons for political officials to associate themselves with media influence (Freedman, 2018).

Instead of just looking at the cause-and-effect links between changes in media ownership and the rise of right-wing populism, this study takes a critical realist approach to look at the structural features of media ownership as possible factors that could help authoritarian populism grow and stay strong. Mechanisms and their effects have a conditional relationship, and their activation is necessary for them to function. This research does not claim that changes in news media ownership structures will always result in authoritarian populism, nor does it imply that authoritarian populism is impossible without these changes. Expanding on previous research, it is argued that media ownership arrangements are more suitable for authoritarian-populist communication when they show high levels of concentration and the potential to isolate and sideline media owners who lack strong affiliations with others. Media ownership characteristics, as mentioned above, contribute to the authoritarian-populist agenda by limiting diverse perspectives in the democratic public sphere and promoting patronage-driven business connections that illustrate the intersection of economic and political power.

Authoritarian Populism in the Sample Countries

This study analyses the evolution of media ownership networks in Hungary and Turkey, where populist governments have held differing degrees of power. It also compares these instances with the Norwegian case to uncover variations in media ownership concentration between hybrid and democratic regimes. The cases were chosen based on two factors: the degree of influence by populist movements during the time period being studied and significant variations in historical, geographical, and cultural features. The analysis concentrated on two instances of hybrid regimes characterized by extended populist influence, along with one democratic regime where a right-wing populist party was partially part of the governing coalition. Furthermore, to strengthen the comparison, cases that exhibited significant differences in terms of historical, geographical, and cultural characteristics were carefully selected. In particular, important factors such as the degree of socio-economic progress and recent historical events were considered. The cases enable us to examine important factors like the prevalence of populist dominance and ownership structures within the media in various scenarios characterized by differences in economic growth and historical context.

Authoritarian populism in Hungary, specifically under Prime Minister Viktor Orbán, is marked by a methodical destruction of democratic structures and the principles of justice, which were initially leveraged to obtain control (Belder, 2023). This political approach involves sustained attacks on the rule of law, civil rights, media freedom, and electoral rules, effectively dismantling key democratic institutions (Belder, 2023). Orbán's regime has used crises such as the economic downturn, the refugee crisis, and the COVID-19 pandemic to intensify conflicts between an illiberal "self" and liberal "others," often framing the EU as a threat to traditional national lifestyles (Krekó & Enyedi, 2018; Scheiring, 2018; Szebeni & Salojärvi, 2022). The regime's economic policies have played a crucial role in democratic erosion, combining expansionary fiscal measures with a punitive workfare system. This approach has concurrently favored oligarchs and foreign investors, leading to social discontent managed through political authoritarianism (Ádám, 2023). The Hungarian example also illustrates the performative elements of populism, employing nation-building and legislation to establish a division between "us" and "them" (Palonen, 2018). The constitutional revisions carried out by the Hungarian government mirror a shift toward a competitive authoritarian system instead of introducing a novel style of constitutional governance, thus eroding fundamental democratic principles (Toth, 2020). The restructuring of the media landscape, including changes in ownership structure, policy, and institutions, played a crucial role in the processes that led to the decline of democracy since 2010 (Bánkuti et al., 2012; Scheiring, 2018). The intricate interaction of populism, nationalism, and authoritarianism has positioned Hungary as not only the primary example of democratic decline in Europe but also an early instance of a hybrid regime within the continent (Batory, 2022; Freedom House, 2023).

Authoritarian populism in Turkey, particularly during the leadership of the Justice and Development Party (AKP) and its leader Recep Tayyip Erdogan, exhibits several distinct characteristics. Initially, the AKP has used religious populism to justify its restrictive regulation of digital technology and media by linking Islamist principles with state policies, thus legitimizing digital authoritarianism and information control (Yilmaz & Erturk, 2021). The AKP's populist policies have transitioned from favoring the majority to embracing neoliberal authoritarianism, signifying a change in its dominant agenda aimed at strengthening control (Yilmaz, 2023). The AKP's initial success was bolstered by a highly favorable macro-political-economic climate. This allowed it to effectively balance the implementation of neoliberal policies with comprehensive social assistance programs aimed at supporting the most vulnerable members of society (Özdemir, 2020). However, as this climate deteriorated, the AKP's populism shifted toward a more authoritarian form, exacerbated by economic crises and the COVID-19 pandemic (Pinar & Gehring, 2023). The AKP has also co-opted the far-right Nationalist Action Party (MHP) to strengthen its authoritarian rule, creating a right-wing populist alliance (Karataşlı & Kumral, 2023). Protests in support of the government and the concentration of media ownership have been utilized by the AKP to showcase widespread backing and quell opposition, thereby reinforcing its authoritarian position (Gümrükçü, 2022). The increase of competitive authoritarianism in Turkey during Erdogan's leadership is characterized by the strategic utilization of religious and identity politics across digital and traditional media platforms, informal legal processes, and incorporating far-right elements to uphold and validate authoritarian dominance (Yilmaz et al., 2021).

Authoritarian populism is also present in the Norwegian political landscape, shaping party dynamics, public discourse, and voter behavior. The Norwegian Progress Party (FrP) demonstrated this influence during their time in a coalition government led by the Conservative Party from 2013 to January 2020. Their approach combined nativist and market-liberal principles, allowing them to confront the center-left government, particularly regarding issues such as high energy prices following the Ukraine invasion (Sunnercrantz, Liv, 2023). The FrP's populist communication approach, defined by its anti-establishment language and restrictive positions on immigration, emphasizes its influence in the political sphere (Thomas, 2020). This populist approach has sparked intense political conflicts, notably between the FrP and the Labor Party, rooted in historical trauma such as the 2011 terror attacks. These conflicts polarize citizens along authoritarian and non-authoritarian lines, with each group rallying behind their respective parties (Berntzen, 2020). The FrP's integration into the political system, facilitated by the absence of a cordon sanitaire, has allowed it to adopt a more moderate stance, enabling coalition governance with the Conservative Party between 2013 and 2020 (Inghammar & Skjønberg, 2023). Authoritarian populism in Norway not only influences party strategies and voter alignments but also sparks broader societal debates on immigration, multiculturalism, and national identity, reflecting similar trends observed across Europe (Bjånesøy, 2023; Naerland, 2016).

Overall, the emergence of authoritarian populism in these countries is often tied to economic and political upheavals; however, the specific expressions and approaches vary. Norway's populism is characterized by conflict-driven polarization and negative partisanship, Turkey's by mass mobilization and symbolic politics, and Hungary's by a systematic dismantling of democratic institutions through ethnonationalist and authoritarian tactics (Bjånesøy, 2023; Bugaric, 2019; Elçi, 2019; Vihma et al., 2021).

Media Outlet Sampling and Data Collection

The sampling of media organizations and companies in this study is based on standardized media-audience measurements wherever possible. Therefore, the sampling unit is media organizations rather than media companies. This study covers all periodical news media organizations in the print (including daily newspapers, weekly magazines, and political journals), online (both online publications and online versions of print publications), and TV and radio sectors, covering both private and public stations. These organizations must have a national audience reach on a daily basis or an average annual market share of at least 3% in 2010, 2016, or 2022. For each of these years, the data refers to the company that owned the broadcasting organization at the end of that year. Ownership or group data were collected through national databases such as business registers and economic archives.

Examining Social Network Structure and Information Flow

Social network analysis makes a crucial observation about the connection between network structure and its informative attributes, particularly in relation to the centralization of networks (Scott, 2017; Scott & Carrington, 2011). Several studies have indicated that a high degree of centralization facilitates efficient dissemination of information within communication networks (Ahuja et al., 2003; Cross & Cummings, 2004; Wallmann & Gerschberger, 2021). Degree centralization quantifies the number of connections that each node possesses within a network (Mendonca et al., 2021; Wasserman & Faust, 1994). In systems with a small number of critical nodes that are highly interconnected, information can spread rapidly and effectively. This architecture enables the efficient and undistorted propagation of messages across the network, granting central nodes significant authority over the messaging process. However, this can also result in these few nodes exerting significant control over the flow of information, potentially leading to bias (Bienenstock & Bonacich, 2022; Wallmann & Gerschberger, 2021).

Some research emphasizes that while these networks are effective in disseminating a particular message, they also have disadvantages. Centralized networks excel at disseminating a singular message but may result in leader isolation and the formation of an "echo chamber," wherein only specific viewpoints are acknowledged, potentially giving rise to biased information and groupthink (Bienenstock & Bonacich, 2022).

When applying these understandings to media ownership networks, attention moves from gathering information to the activities of spreading and transmitting information. The main focus is not on the biases that occur during the collection of information but rather on the biases that are introduced when the information is distributed. The primary concern in this situation is how network architecture affects the control media owners have over messaging and how this control impacts the variety of perspectives presented. In media ownership networks, centralized structures mean that a few media owners can control the messages being broadcast, which can reduce the variety of opinions and influence public perception (Baker, 2006; Gilens & Hertzman, 2000).

This research aims to establish the extent of influence held by central nodes within a network. A high level of eigenvector centralization signifies that these central nodes exert an unevenly significant impact on the network, potentially leading to biased information diffusion (Bonacich, 2007). The notion of eigenvector centralization aids in the identification of the most influential nodes within a network by taking into account not only their direct connections but also the connections of their neighbors, thus demonstrating their overall impact within the network (Iacobucci et al., 2018). High eigenvector centralization scores indicate that a small number of central nodes exert a disproportionate effect, rendering the network susceptible to domination by disconnected elites and diminishing the diversity of perspectives (Bonacich, 2007). Within media ownership networks, the presence of common ownership frequently results in the dissemination of similar content across several outlets. This can be attributed to the utilization of shared resources or driven by political reasons, ultimately leading to a reduction in the availability of diverse information. Media networks with high eigenvector centralization demonstrate significant dominance by central media businesses in controlling the accessible information, potentially suppressing peripheral voices and diminishing media diversity (Metz & Neri, 2021). This paper examines the application of these principles to networks of media ownership. It demonstrates that alterations in the structure of these networks can impact the concentration of ownership and the diversity of media outlets. Specifically, central nodes within the network exert greater control over the content of messages.

Results

The research examines the media ownership structure in Hungary, Turkey, and Norway for the years 2010, 2016, and 2022 by employing standard network visualization methods in R (graph package). The most common structural network characteristics are calculated, including the number of components, the size of the main component, and the average degree. In addition to evaluating network density metrics and the prevalent measure of centralization using Freeman degree centrality, we also computed the distribution of eigenvector centralization scores for each year and network following Bienenstock and Bonacich's (2022) methodology (Bienenstock & Bonacich, 2022). Collectively, these measures allow us to comprehensively describe changes in network structure and understand their impact on ownership concentration, media pluralism, and the overall dynamics of the industry.

Upon initial examination of the network visualization, two prevalent patterns were observed in nearly all instances (refer to Figures: 3.1–3.3 in Appendix) Upon initial examination of the network visualization, two prevalent patterns were observed in nearly all instances (refer to Figures: 3.1–3.3 in Appendix). Firstly, there was a consistent rise in the number of "nodes" within the network over the observation period.

Secondly, large components in the form of sub-graphs of connected nodes are especially noticeable in the cases of Hungary and Turkey. This clear signal implies a focus on ownership among specific media corporations across different media platforms. The size of the two largest components, i.e., the largest connected sub-network, increases significantly between 2010 and 2022 for Hungary, while it shows a decreasing trend in Turkey during the decade leading up to 2020 but a relatively increasing trend after 2020. The size of the top two components increased over time. For instance, in Hungary, it grew from 17 nodes in 2010 to 32 in 2016, and further to 76 in 2022. In Norway, the media landscape was characterized by a high degree of market concentration (Figure 3.3 in Appendix), and the number of components slightly decreased between 2010 and 2022, albeit not noticeably (Figure 3.4). Between 2010 and 2022, the number of components in Hungary showed a steady increase (Figure 3.5). In Turkey, the number of components also increased, although not as rapidly as in Hungary.

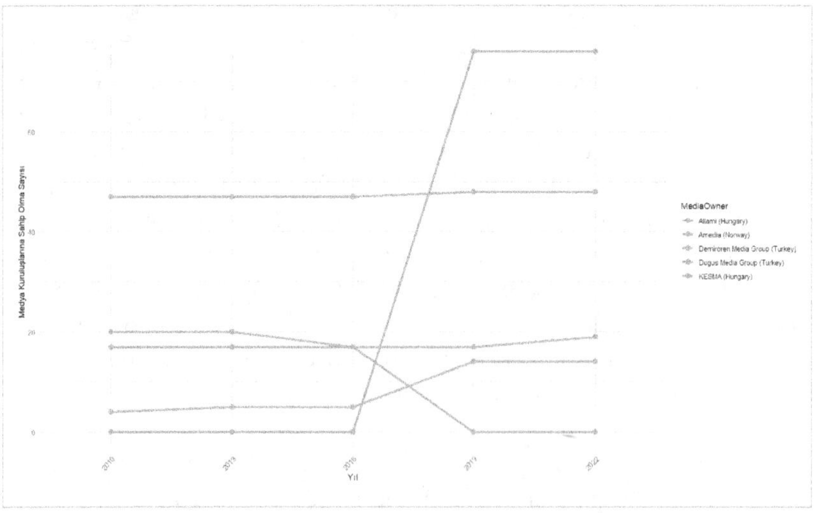

Figure 3.4. The Size of Largest Two Components 2010–2022

At first sight, this may suggest a rise in media variety in Turkey and Norway and a growth in consolidation in Hungary. A decrease in the proportion of marginal nodes, specifically those with just one or two links, was noted in Hungary. The number of marginal nodes in Hungary decreased from 79 percent in 2010 to 74 percent in 2020, while in Turkey the number of marginal nodes remained relatively stable, ranging between 88 percent in 2010 and 89 percent in 2020. A similar situation is observed in the case of Norway. Independence from centralized nodes may be suggested by marginality. As a result, the decrease in the number of marginal nodes observed across all countries could indicate a growing integration of networks and consequently an increased influence of centralized nodes on the diffusion of information.

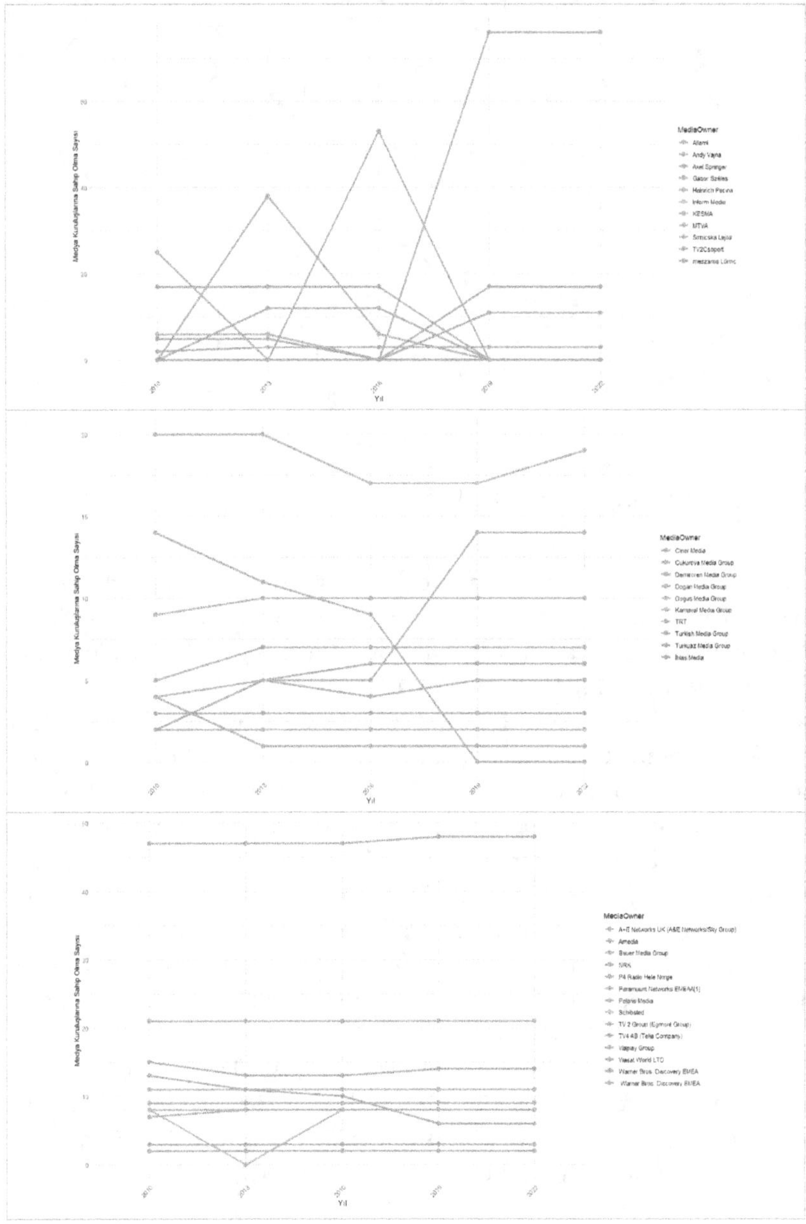

Figure 3.5. Number of Components 2010–2022

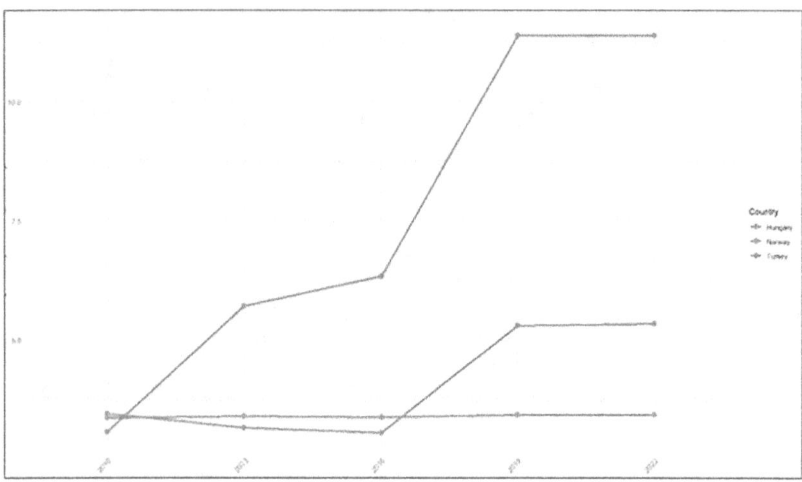

Figure 3.6. Mean Degree 2010–2022

The study subsequently focused on examining more advanced indicators of network integration, with particular emphasis on measures of connection. We computed the mean degree, which is defined as the average number of linkages per node, for every network and year (Figure 3.6). The trends vary among countries. Between 2010 and 2020, Hungary witnessed a consistent growth in network connectivity, followed by a period of stabilization after 2020. In contrast, Turkey and Norway maintained a relatively stable number of connections, particularly from 2010 to 2022. The smaller sample countries have a higher number of ties per node compared to Turkey, which has a larger media market. This pattern is logical, as networks that have a greater number of nodes generally have a lower density. Collectively, the connectivity metric can be understood as showing networks with progressively stronger connections in Hungary, although this is not true for Norway and Turkey.

To examine if there have been any alterations in media ownership arrangements that may result in the rise of authoritarian populism, we utilized the methodology suggested by Bienenstock and Bonacich (2022). Within this framework, we initially computed eigenvector centralization scores for each individual network.

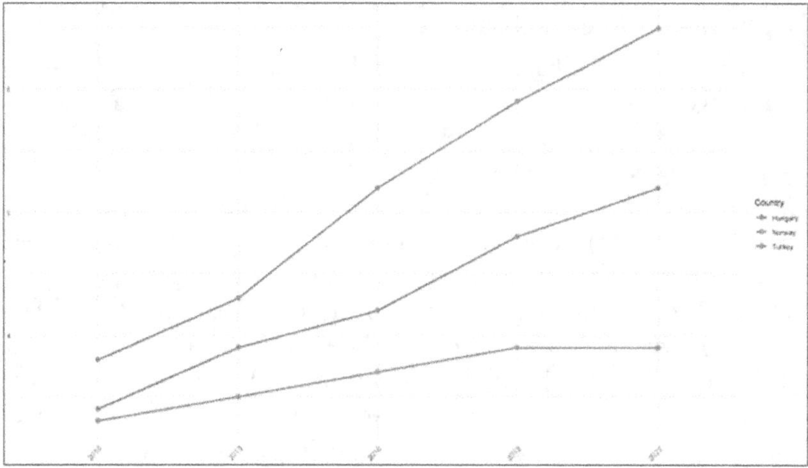

Figure 3.7. Eigenvector Centralization 2010–2022

The data presented in Figure 3.7 indicates that from 2010 to 2022, the level of eigenvector centralization remained generally consistent in Norway, Hungary, and Turkey. Nevertheless, as of 2019, there has been a rise in eigenvector centralization across all countries. Hungary experienced the most significant rise, while Turkey also achieved substantially greater levels of eigenvector centralization in 2019 compared to earlier decades.

Norway experienced the smallest growth between 2010 and 2022. The significant fluctuations in scores are likely attributable to the emergence of a novel form of organization (online news organizations), which may have originally caused disruption to the established media network structure. However, over the next ten years, there was a significant rise in the diversity of networks in all instances. This aligns with the notion that the core became more robust while the outlying regions became less interconnected. This could indicate the assimilation of online media into established media conglomerates. Nevertheless, it is intriguing to observe the varying degrees of disruption and reintegration that have occurred. Indeed, the center-periphery difference has only been apparent in the last decade in the examples of Hungary and Turkey.

Discussion and Conclusion

Extensive media research highlights the political significance of media ownership (Bagdikiian, 2004; Baker, 2006; Freedman, 2018; McChesney, 2000b, 2000a; Meier & Trappel, 2007; Mosco, 1996) This paper conceptualizes that news media ownership structures significantly contribute to the emergence and consolidation of authoritarian populism when heavily centralized and tend to marginalize peripheral media owners around a particular outlet. These arrangements promote the amplification of messages from highly centralized actors while suppressing those from less centralized ones. The study has shown that these two tendencies have been particularly pronounced in Hungary and Turkey, hybrid regimes where authoritarian-populist structures have been in place over the last 12 years. In contrast, Norway, with its democratic mechanisms, has seen an increase in populist discourse.

The use of measures to assess the informational effects of network structures reveals that connectivity, as measured by average degree, has evolved in slightly different ways in Hungary and Turkey. In Hungary, there has been a significant increase in the number of connections, whereas in Turkey, it shows a more consistent linear pattern with a lower rate of increase. In the case of Norway, a much more consistent linear pattern is observed compared to Turkey. Nonetheless, with regards to assortative (see Figure 7.1) and the consequent dominance of central nodes over peripheral nodes, there is evidence of a rise in network structures across all countries from 2010 to 2022. This implies that the most centralized elements in the network can enhance their influence over the information shared across the media network. This is demonstrated by the rise in assortative across nearly all situations, though at varying degrees, as well as the reduction in peripheral nodes, which may reveal a trend of "silencing opposing viewpoints." The reduction in marginal nodes might suggest a decrease in the variety of views and opinions and a limited exchange of conflicting perspectives within the media environments under analysis. In this context, it is worth observing the advancements in Hungary and Turkey as prime examples of influential right-wing populism. These two countries experienced the most significant rise in central-peripheral inequality compared to the situation in 2010. Norway has also experienced an increase, although it is not as pronounced as in the other two countries, mainly due to the shift from traditional print media to digital formats. It is evident that the significant rise in center-periphery structures is not merely a result of the growing incorporation of online sources into media environments. While this study does not allow for direct proof of the strategic aims of populist governments, consistent observations and patterns suggest such an explanation.

Secondly, there has been a general trend toward greater diversity and a larger number of media organizations because of the emergence of an increasing number of private channels and online sources. This has led to more interconnected networks between 2010 and 2022 in Hungary and, to a lesser extent, in Turkey. Network connectivity has only stabilized in Norway between 2010 and 2022. (Figure 3.6). From a purely graph theory perspective, this discovery is intuitive because the addition of new nodes generally results in more disorganized networks. This is especially true for large networks, as they typically have relatively fewer connections between nodes (Scott & Carrington, 2011; Wasserman & Faust, 1994). Under an authoritarian-populist political environment, it is contended that tightly concentrated media ownership setups lead to increasingly close ties between economic, political, and media elites. This situation may hinder the media's role as a "watchdog" and strengthen clientelist relationships between the media and policymakers.

The research demonstrates that in situations like Turkey and Hungary, where there are populist authoritarian systems in place, the ownership of media has changed to create favorable circumstances for communication supporting authoritarian populism. Given that Hungary and Turkey are widely known as extreme instances of authoritarian populism, it could be anticipated that the media ownership markets in these two nations would be entirely centralized and under government authority. Nevertheless, the findings indicate that a certain level of diversity in media ownership endures. As a result, there is no significant decrease in the number of components in networks, and the size of the largest components does not experience substantial growth in any country. Consequently, we would anticipate a higher level of ownership concentration in Turkey and Hungary. At the furthest extreme, nearly every element overseen by a lone proprietor might have vanished. The continued presence of diverse components in these two countries, from an ownership perspective, may suggest that there are still several formally independent media groups in these countries. The fact that the ownership networks are not fully interconnected indicates that these regimes have not yet completely succumbed to a closed authoritarian regime.

It also reveals their parallel character with the definition of competitive authoritarian regimes, which is a subcategory of hybrid regimes. In other words, these nations do not attempt to entirely abolish the structures of the democratic public arena. Instead, they aim to maintain some appearance of democratic rivalry. This is why they are labeled as competitive authoritarian regimes. (Levitsky and Way, 2002). Nevertheless, by employing more advanced methods to analyze center-periphery structures, such as eigenvector centralization scores, the research also indicates that complete ownership control might not be essential for right-wing authoritarians to exert their desired influence over public discourse. Graph theory and social network analysis indicate that strong assortative, particularly in the instances of Hungary and Turkey, can effectively suppress opposing viewpoints. Such structures enable right-wing populists to maintain a level of dissenting voices that allows them to assert their support for media freedom while also permitting some critical perspectives to exist. This may align with the divisive populist strategy of identifying internal enemies without compromising control over media content. According to Bruff's research on authoritarian populism, there is evidence of authoritarianism in the reorganization of state and institutional power with the goal of protecting specific policies and institutional procedures from social and political resistance (Bruff, 2014). The merging and intertwining of political and economic power, such as the concentration of media ownership, indicates an authoritarian restructuring that maintains a facade of pluralism but ultimately ensures government control over the media.

While network analysis alone does not enable us to make direct inferences about the motivations behind structural changes or their influence on real media diversity and dialogue, some informal evidence could aid in understanding our findings. This is evident through notable variations in how populists utilize these structures between a democratic scenario where one moderate populist discourse predominates partially and a hybrid regime scenario with two robust populist dominances.

In Norway, media ownership is characterized by a high degree of regulation aimed at sustaining democracy and freedom of speech through diversity in output and plurality in ownership, driven by concerns over the influence of powerful media owners on content (Sjøvaag, 2014). This regulatory framework aims to mitigate the influence of owners on content, thereby maintaining a democratic media system. Nevertheless the Norwegian media landscape was characterized by a high degree of market concentration, with significant control held by a few dominant firms (Sjøvaag, 2012). This trend was consistent with global patterns. The concentration of media ownership also raised questions about its impact on pluralism and diversity, a concern echoed globally (Winseck, 2022). The Norwegian press has historically been influenced by political affiliations, with the party press system evolving due to electoral mobilization and economic progress, although recent trends show a shift toward simpler mass communication structures driven by audience-market dynamics and advertising strategies (Vaagan, 2008). The evolution of media ownership in Norway during this period reflects a broader trend of market-driven consolidation, tempered by regulatory efforts to balance economic and democratic imperatives. This dynamic interplay between market forces and regulatory frameworks underscores the complexity of media ownership in a digitally advanced and economically robust country like Norway (Galetić et al., 2016; Höyer, 1968; Sjøvaag & Krumsvik, 2018). The Norwegian state's media policy has attempted to balance political, cultural, and economic interests, but the increasing focus on profitability among media outlets challenges this balance (Østerud & Selle, 2006). Disruptive events, such as the Oslo terror attack, have also shown that media can alter public discourse significantly, challenging mainstream definitions of appropriateness and deviance (Larsson & Skogerbø, 2018). Furthermore, the experiences of politicians subjected to scandalizing media exposure highlight the media's power in shaping political narratives and the personal and professional repercussions for those involved (Figenschou & Beyer, 2014). Overall, the concentration of media ownership in Norway has led to a more economically driven media environment, which influences political discourse by prioritizing profitability and engagement over political diversity and local democratic processes. This contrasts sharply with the media environments in Hungary and Turkey, where concentrated media ownership has facilitated the rise and endurance of authoritarian populism. The cases of Hungary and Turkey make it plausible to draw a clear link between the stability and continuity of the authoritarian-populist regime and the increasing concentration of ownership structures. Orbán and Erdoğan not only benefited from concentrated media ownership structures but also actively redesigned the media structure in order to control the flow of information during their time in office. For example, Fidesz-affiliated media outlets are known to publish the same headlines and content both in print and online (Rényi, 2019). This was made possible by Orban, whose strategy aims to use state advertising practices as a critical tool for governments to influence media content. This practice has led to a media environment where ownership is closely tied to political patronage, ensuring that media outlets align with government interests. The concentration of media ownership in Hungary was not limited to print media but extended to radio and other forms of news dissemination, with significant political implications, especially around election periods (Earle et al., 2005). The Hungarian public's news consumption patterns also reflected this concentration, with a notable polarization and the prevalence of information bubbles, where consumers were exposed predominantly to views from one political side (B. J. Birkinbine & Gómez, 2020). Similarly, in Turkey, the ruling elites exert control over information flows through access restrictions, legal cases, and attacks on media companies, effectively privatizing governance and aligning media with state interests. The Turkish media landscape is characterized by a high degree of political polarization, with media outlets divided into pro-government and opposition camps, reflecting the broader democracy-authoritarianism cleavage in Turkish politics (Yanatma, 2021). While Hungary's media ownership concentration is more state-driven, Turkey's is influenced by a combination of corporate interests and political clientelism, resulting in a media environment that is highly susceptible to government influence and economic pressures.

Thus, while Norway's concentrated but regulated media ownership fosters a balanced and democratic flow of information, Hungary and Turkey's concentrated media ownership facilitates control by competitive authoritarian regimes, restricting information diversity, undermining democratic processes, and providing fertile ground for the rise and endurance of authoritarian populism. This study provides important evidence that media ownership structures have become favorable for authoritarian politics in Hungary and Turkey, while in Norway it has been shown how democratic structures and institutions have made them unfavorable.

Subsequent research should thoroughly investigate the intentional methods, motives, and procedures employed by various individuals or groups to reorganize media ownership. Given that news media ownership concentration is a prevalent phenomenon worldwide (Noam et al., 2016), it is imperative for scholars to focus on the national political circumstances that contribute to this concentration. Furthermore, as our data solely focuses on official ownership connections and disregards informal connections like political or familial associations, further investigation is required to qualitatively reveal the informal connections between media owners and authoritarian populists, as well as their impact on editorial decisions.

NATO and "Peace Technology" for Human Security

Esra Albayrakoğlu

ABSTRACT

In an era where technology is increasingly weaponized, Peace Technology stands out as an emerging field that uses technology as a force for good. Against the growing tide of traditional and non-traditional challenges, many of which directly and negatively affect humans, Peace Technology aims to prevent, mitigate, and eliminate online and offline threats through innovative research and development. Its mission is to utilize science to anticipate tensions, preclude escalation, encourage dialogue via "techplomacy" and contribute to sustainable development for positive peace. By using cutting-edge technology, NATO has been investing in human security and advancing the resilience of home and partner populations for more than two decades. In this vein, NATO has adopted a multi-vectored perspective to protect civilians, the natural environment, civilian infrastructure, and cultural property in peacetime, crises, and conflicts. This chapter introduces the audience to the origins and history of Peace Technology, offers examples of technology used for early warning for violence prevention, digital diplomacy, and smart city development, and discusses the obstacles and opportunities associated with Peace Technology by evaluating NATO's activities as a case study.

Keywords: Human Security, NATO, Peace, Peace Technology

Introduction

Technology has always been a double-edged sword, featuring both perils and promises. Throughout the centuries, various civilian and military technologies have inflicted harm to advance selfish interests, while other technologies have served the public good by increasing the quality of life. Today, there is a growing emphasis on investing in Peace Technology as a collective action toward transforming the world where people shall live without need and fear. In Johan Galtung's terms, this refers to "positive peace" which means more than the mere "absence of direct violence between states" (Galtung & Fischer, 2013, p. 173).

The United Nations Development Program's (UNDP) Human Development Report of 1994 defines "Human Security" as complementary to other dimensions of security by "prioritizing the people." This statement not only treats the security of people on par with that of states but also highlights the importance of "interdependence among people, and between people and planet" against the backdrop of the United Nations (UN) 2030 Agenda for Sustainable Development (UNDP, 2022).

In an increasingly anthropocentric world, this holistic perspective calls for solidarity to tackle the cross-border, tech-based, and network-centric challenges in modern times. For example, every species on earth is vulnerable or sensitive to climate-related biodegradation, cyber insecurity, violent extremism, and illicit trafficking of arms, drugs, and humans, among others. These problems often spill over to the economy and politics, thereby eroding state and societal resilience. Nevertheless, even though humans are fallible and prone to making mistakes, they may also draw lessons from them and act as changemakers with the help of technological innovations.

Premised on the values and principles of the UN's founding charter, the North Atlantic Treaty Organization (NATO) is a political alliance even though its military role was paramount in the Cold War years. Although initially established in 1949 as a military bulwark against the communist threat, it began diversifying its security agenda in the post-Cold War years to gradually move away from nuclear issues toward energy and environmental security, migration issues, and resilience. Rather than becoming obsolete once the archenemy Soviet Union was gone, NATO intensified an adaptation process that had already started toward the end of the Cold War. From the early 2000s onwards, NATO has accorded an ever-increasing importance to bringing order, stability, and prosperity in its geography and beyond by broadening the notion of national security. The idea that the abuse of human rights could "lead to crises affecting Euro-Atlantic stability," the Alliance adopted "humanitarian intervention" in its agenda as exemplified in its operations in Kosovo (March-June 1999) and Libya (2011). Its non-combat roles in the Global Coalition to Defeat Daesh/ISIS also stemmed from a concern for civilians bearing the brunt of this violent extremist organization (Leonardis, 2023, pp. 4–16).

In NATO's terms, Human Security pertains to "risks and threats to populations where NATO has operations, missions or activities" in peacetime, crisis and conflict contexts. By emphasizing human dignity and inalienable human rights, NATO distinguishes itself from authoritarian state and non-state rivals, who continuously breach basic liberties. Woven through all these areas is a gender perspective based on the UN's Women, Peace and Security

Agenda of 2000 (NATO, August 30, 2024). Even though NATO is engaged in military technologies for operational effectiveness, it also invests heavily in other technologies to save human lives, minimize danger to infrastructure, and create peacetime and post-conflict resilience.

Nexus Between Human and Security and Peace Technology

War and technology have always been a part of the human condition. As "the application of science to produce useful things," engineering has served defensive and offensive policies designed by rulers. Both military and civilian engineering can be dated to ancient times. Military engineers helped policymakers by advancing weaponry and defense structures for the national interest, while civilian engineers sought to upgrade countries' infrastructure to uplift humans' living and working standards. The line between the two kinds of engineering is always blurred, since a technology emanating from the civilian sector may inspire the military establishment or vice versa (Vesilind, 2010, pp. 4–12). Over the past few decades "a third kind of engineering career" has been introduced by engineers willing to serve the public good and contribute meaningfully to peace and justice. According to Vesilind (2010, p. 12):

> These engineers recognize that military engineering, in all its forms, including working for defense contractors and conducting research for the Department of Defense, is destined to be used for warfare, either defensive or offensive, and they are unsure if they want to participate in such work. Engineers in the civilian sector might question if their skills and talents are being used in the best way possible. Is the design and construction of another big-box superstore, for example, really the best way to spend limited global resources? Some military and civilian engineers are looking for alternatives that would allow them to use their engineering skills in a positive and proactive way to promote peace and justice. These engineers, by their actions, are defining a third kind of engineering—peace engineering.

Peace engineers have introduced "Peace Technology" or "PeaceTech" as a novel field of research and practice. In this context, technology transforms into a tool by playing a "co-constitutive role in peacebuilding." Artificial Intelligence (AI), Augmented Reality, Virtual Reality, geospatial technologies, and many others can be utilized to support peace and peace-related causes around the world like awareness raising campaigns, human rights monitoring, diplomacy, war crimes evidence collection, humanitarian assistance, disaster relief, climate adaptation and cultural heritage preservation (Glybchenko, 2024, pp. 117–118).

Peace Technology incorporates software and hardware to help predict, prevent, mitigate, and eliminate online and offline challenges to humans. It relates to products and services for capacity building, fact-checking, inter-communal dialogue, early warning of conflicts, post-conflict rehabilitation, and sustainable development. Various universities and non-governmental organizations (NGOs) collaborate with intergovernmental organizations (IGOs) to create safe, secure, and prosperous environments for people. While institutions like the University of Ulster (InPeaceLab) and European University Institute (Global PeaceTech Hub) feature the "research and development" (R&D) component of this collaboration, humanitarian non-profit NGOs like Build Up prove to be the eyes and ears on the ground, mapping the conflict terrain to provide data for various peace projects and act as facilitators, suppliers, and mediators. Among the IGOs, the United Nations stands out as an innovator and enabler based on its Strategy for the Digital Transformation of UN Peacekeeping. Likewise, the Digital Innovation Cell within the Department of Political and Peacebuilding Affairs is heavily engaged in Peace Technology. This unit's interdisciplinary team aims to "understand and explore, pilot, and scale new technologies, tools, and practices in conflict prevention, mediation, and peacebuilding" (Bell, 2024, pp. 14–15, 69–74).

Many landmark outputs of Peace Technology belong to the UN, with occasional joint work with various start-ups like Remesh. "AI-powered conversational bots to enable peacebuilding in war zones" have enabled tech-assisted dialogue to broker peace among communities in Libya and Yemen. "Machine learning to survey infrastructure damage," developed by the UNDP, features an algorithm to identify and categorize war-damaged infrastructure for post-conflict reconstruction. Created by the United Nations Population Fund (UNPF), a "common operational dataset" for humanitarian partners working in Ukraine provides updated population projections based on age, gender, and region within the country. It has also served as open-source information about casualties, refugees, and funding requirements to assist vulnerable and displaced people within Ukraine (Davletov, Kalkar, Ragnet, & Verhulst, 2022, pp. 13–15).

For its part, NATO also embraced a more comprehensive approach to peace and security in the post-Cold War era. The end of nuclear competition meant that non-traditional threats like "environmental disasters, terrorist organizations, and unexpected population movements" have replaced traditional state-based threats. Since these threats may render precautionary state measures ineffective, they pave the way to human insecurity. There is a growing awareness about state or national security not being equivalent to human security, as sometimes the state apparatus may fail to safeguard or arbitrarily work against the best interests of its citizens. In this respect, "Human Security" offers "a holistic, evolving, people-centric interpretation of security that exists when an individual has political and civil rights (freedom from fear) and social and economic rights (freedom from want)." In a conflict or post-conflict scenario, simply focusing on counterterrorism or counterinsurgency along with state reconstruction and recovery might be self-defeating. In the case of NATO, even if the Alliance is not and cannot be the leader in uplifting the living and working standards of people in distress, capacity building in collaboration with the relevant humanitarian organizations that have the primary mandate for this task is vital for mission effectiveness and credibility. This was significantly lacking in NATO's policy in Afghanistan after the 9/11 attacks against the USA in 2001:

> NATO was seeking to address traditional security concerns (protecting the member states from attacks through hard military power) without really appreciating the need for a strong human security (helping to remove the conditions that many in the alliance believed facilitate the rise of Al-Qaeda and the Taliban in Afghanistan) component (Kfir, 2015, pp. 223–226).

Human Security and Nato's Transformation

First mentioned in the Wales Summit Declaration in 2014 "as a topic of practical cooperation with partners to address common security threats," "Human Security" began to occupy an increasingly larger space since the Brussels Summit in 2021. For NATO, Human Security refers to the risks and threats to civilians and objects of cultural heritage, environment, and infrastructure that render their lives meaningful. While most deliberate harm against civilians stems from belligerent acts, NATO forces may also inflict unintended harm on civilians during missions, operations, and activities. The multiple strands of Human Security from NATO's standpoint are as follows: "Protection of Civilians (PoC); Protection of Children in Armed Conflict (CAAC); Combating Trafficking in Human Beings (CTHB); Conflict-related Sexual Violence (CRSV), and Cultural Property Protection (CPP)." They also pair well with NATO's adoption of the UN's Women, Peace and Security (WPS) Agenda, which aims at women's visibility and empowerment across the Alliance's three core tasks (NATO, August 30, 2024).

NATO's latest Strategic Concept adopted at the Madrid Summit in 2022 signifies a milestone in NATO's history with its reference to Human Security for the first time and emphasis on "the cross-cutting importance of investing in human security and the Women, Peace and Security agenda across all core tasks." It also features a revision of the three core tasks: Deterrence and defense (mentioned as "collective defense" in the 2010 Concept), crisis prevention and management ("crisis management" in the 2010 Concept), and cooperative security. The emphasis is now on taking more preventive measures in the name of Human Security and dealing with the disease rather than the symptoms (NATO, June 29, 2022).

NATO 2022 Strategic Concept followed another important document titled Human Security: Approach and Guiding Principles. It aims to "provide a coherent and consistent understanding of Human Security for NATO." Acknowledging that conflict is increasingly fought in "spaces inseparable from civilian populations" and that they are "being deliberately targeted in conflict," the text calls for "prevention and protection oriented" actions for operational effectiveness and sustainable peace and security (NATO, October 14, 2022).

At every step of its planning and implementation, Human Security calls for a gender-responsive, victim-centered, and trauma-informed approach. As wars are increasingly fought in or near civilian settlements, it is indispensable to adopt human-oriented policies to prevent, respond to, and stop urban warfare. This is well-illustrated by indiscriminate targeting of civilians and critical infrastructure along with documented torture, sexual abuse, and deliberate destruction of cultural property by Russia in the Ukrainian territory, violent extremist organizations like ISIS in the Middle East and Africa, or during the mutual offenses in Gaza (Rosén, 2023; NATO CCOE, 2023; NATO CCOE, 2024).

According to Lepskiy and Lepska, the war in Ukraine showcased "the incompetence of major world security institutions" requiring a transition "from peacekeeping and peacebuilding to peace engineering." (2023, pp. 402–403). NATO had already been undergoing this process, which was further accelerated in the light of Russian atrocities, culminating in "the 360-degree approach" across all domains and directions and against all threats and challenges (NATO, June 29, 2022). The Alliance is mindful of the link between Human Security and Emerging and Disruptive Technologies (EDTs), like Autonomous Weapon Systems manufactured or acquired by state and non-state perpetrators. The *2022 Strategic Concept* acknowledges the pros and cons of EDTs as they radically change the nature of conflict. NATO members have concurred to "promote innovation and increase investments in EDTs to retain NATO's interoperability and military edge" together with the private sector, and fully complying with principles of responsible use premised upon "the Alliance's democratic values and human rights" (NATO, August 8, 2024).

Deliberated at the 2021 Brussels Summit and launched in 2022, the Defense Innovation Accelerator for the North Atlantic (DIANA) has the mission to "foster transatlantic cooperation on critical technologies, promote interoperability and harness civilian innovation" through joint work with academia and the private sector. DIANA utilizes deep-tech, dual-use technological tools to solve competitive defense and security challenges. Its second set of challenges shared in July 2024 belong to areas directly related to Human Security: "Energy & Power; Data & Information Security; Sensing & Surveillance; Human Health & Performance, and Critical Infrastructure & Logistics." Solutions enhancing resilience and support environment-friendly technologies are welcome (NATO, July 1, 2024; NATO, August 8, 2024).

The Washington Summit on July 9–11, 2024, once again condemned Russia as bearing the "sole responsibility for its war of aggression against Ukraine, a blatant violation of international law, including the UN Charter." Pointing at "Russian forces and officials' violations of human rights and war crimes," the document reassures that impunity should not be allowed to continue as thousands of civilians die and the civilian infrastructure is extensively damaged. Russia is also blamed for "its aggressive hybrid actions against Allies, including through proxies" including, but not limited to "sabotage, acts of violence, provocations at Allied borders, instrumentalization of irregular migration, malicious cyber activities, electronic interference, disinformation campaigns, and malign political influence, as well as economic coercion" (NATO, July 10, 2024b). Concomitantly, NATO announced its AI Strategy on

July 10, promising to use AI-assisted technologies in "a safe and responsible way" to deal with spoilers of peace. For the first time, the new strategy defines "AI-enabled disinformation, information operations, and gender-based violence as issues of concern for the Alliance, our societies and democracies" (NATO, July 10, 2024a).

This matches with NATO's ethical leadership as evidenced by its "biotech and human enhancement technologies," reflecting the anticipated impact on defense and security of biotech-related innovations. NATO's "informed, value-based and gender-aware strategy" on biotechnology rests upon the Alliance's defensive posture. It contributes to Human Security by developing biosensors to help detect biological and chemical threats as well as biomaterials to protect and heal servicemen and women (NATO, April 12, 2024).

NATO's Science for Peace and Security Program

NATO members' cooperation dynamics in science and technology have their roots in Article 2 of the Alliance's founding treaty. The Science for Peace and Security (SPS) Program dates to 1957, when "The Three Wise Men," namely the Canadian, Italian, and Norwegian foreign ministers, called for joint efforts "in the non-military field to foster ties among civilian communities of the Alliance" (NATO, June 18, 2019). Science is paramount as the "third dimension" to bring together NATO's military and political identities for defense and development purposes. It is against this background that NATO could play a transformative role in Western Europe by championing science in international relations from the Cold War onwards (NATO, August 8, 2017).

In line with the Women, Peace and Security Agenda, NATO acknowledges the slow progress of women's representation in Science, Technology, Engineering and Mathematics worldwide. For this reason, distinguished women researchers from NATO members and partner countries enjoy equal opportunity and receive support from the SPS Program to contribute solutions to emerging security challenges (NATO, February 11, 2024).

The SPS Program bridges the scientific community and NATO to collaborate on research, innovation, and knowledge exchange to tackle novel challenges. SPS activities enable the Alliance to recognize, define, and combat risks and threats targeting states and humans. The Program also brings together experts and officials from NATO member and partner countries to deliver tangible and meaningful results in the name of scientific advancement to respond to common concerns. Network-building events and projects help people brainstorm solutions related to "cyber defense, counterterrorism, energy and environmental security, and defense against CBRNE agents" (NATO, April 17, 2023).

As early as the 1960s, NATO recognized the security implications of environmental change. Toward the end of this decade, NATO established a scientific research unit named the Committee on the Challenges of Modern Society (CCMS) to concentrate on defense-related environmental issues. The year 2006 marked the point when the SPS Program incorporated the CCMS to promote knowledge exchange and practical teamwork between NATO members and partner states. One of the earliest examples of such "techplomacy" was an SPS project in 2009, bringing together researchers at the Hashemite University of Jordan, Ben-Gurion University in Israel, and the University of Colorado to develop desalination technology, which then "strengthened NATO's presence in the region and, for a short period, cooperation across Middle Eastern states" (Al-Marashi & Causevic, 2020, pp. 36, 39).

Some projects under the auspices of the SPS Program are related to mine clearance in humanitarian operations. Landmines left buried underground in post-conflict environments not only cause innocent casualties but also soil degradation in mine-contaminated areas. For example, decades after the catastrophic Bosnian War of 1995, Bosnia and Herzegovina (BiH) still suffers from "landmines, cluster munitions and other explosive and toxic remnants of war" economically, socially, and environmentally, thus negatively affecting one-quarter of all communities in this country. Accordingly, one SPS project features the new dual sensor ALIS, which combines a metal detector and a ground penetrating radar to assist humanitarian demining activities in BiH. As a time-saving device that also puts operators out of harm's way, ALIS visualizes buried landmines on a PC screen to enable the operator to distinguish mines from other metal particles (NATO, December 2020).

In 2014, a two-year NATO SPS Project called "Best Practices for Cultural Property Protection in NATO-led Military Operations" highlighted the urgency of calling for immediate action in the face of cultural property destruction. Maintaining that the twenty-first-century wars put the cultural property on target as part of identity-based hybrid warfare taking place in urban settlements, the project drew attention to a broad transnational market for looted illicit antiquities, generating revenue, mainly for extremist armed groups (Rosén, 2017, pp. 9–10). Published under the NATO SPS Series, *The Safety and Security of Cultural Heritage in Zones of War or Instability* is a compilation of papers delivered at the online NATO Advanced Research Workshop on November 25–27, 2020, entitled "Cultural heritage's safety and security in zones of war or instability." The Alliance upholds cultural property protection as a core value. It acknowledges that "the illicit trade in antiquities and archaeological finds represents another danger to cultural heritage and can help to finance the terrorist groups." Accordingly, this NATO event sought to find safe and ethical means to safeguard cultural heritage in war zones from belligerent parties. One paper covers ENEA's optical sensors for local and remote sensing of cultural heritage, to "define state-of-the-art conservation, guide restoration, and explore new opportunities in virtual and augmented realities where other complementary information can be merged." Non-destructive and non-invasive, ENEA's combat-proven laser-based sensors display a variety of spectroscopic techniques to deliver information in real-time (NATO, January 14, 2022).

Global pandemics also constituted an agenda item for the NATO SPS Program as a "threat multiplier." Draining the capital as well as the human capital of member and partner states, COVID-19 was a litmus test in terms of resilience. Thus, "the scientific arm of NATO" engaged with scientists and research centers since the onset of this cross-border threat to develop ways and means to halt the virus' spread and diagnose and treat patients (Causevic & Al-Marashi, 2023, p. 74). At a time when states around the world were absorbed with national fervor to keep medical solutions and supplies to themselves, NATO once again tried to revive the spirit of humanity through another act of "techplomacy."

Russian atrocities in Ukraine, disruptive technologies, and climate-related environmental degradation have accelerated collaboration and solidarity within the NATO scientific community. During 2023, the SPS Program supported approximately 100 multi-year R&D projects and welcomed about 250 proposals for novel activities. These endeavors have built and nurtured partnerships to deliver outputs aligned with Allied priorities. Parenthetically, Ukraine stands out as the foremost beneficiary of the SPS Program since the annexation of Crimea in 2014, and dialogue with this country has risen exponentially following Russia's all-out invasion in February 2022. NATO projects assist Ukraine also in "energy security" and "digital resilience" (NATO, April 19, 2024). As an exemplary case, the NATO SPS Advanced Research Workshop "A gender lens approach to military to civilian transition and reintegration for Ukraine Joint Forces Operation women combatants" underscored the importance of women's participation in military service as equal peers to be followed by their healthy reintegration to civilian life. In the context of this (Military to Civilian Transition) research, key priority areas centered on how women undergo post-traumatic stress disorder and other mental health conditions as they return home from conflict zones (NATO, November 4, 2021).

Dated 2023, the "DIMLAB: Deployable CB analytical laboratory" multi-year project involving Spain, Morocco, and Tunisia addressed "chemical-and biological-related risks within the context of both conventional and hybrid warfare." Standing for "detection, identification and monitoring laboratories," DIMLABs are affordable, lightweight, and deployable field labs to offer "swift and accurate identification and diagnosis." In another suitable example Jordan, Morocco, and the UK joined forces for the project "RESCUE: Sensors for early warning of natural disasters." Based on Early Warning Systems (EWSs) "to predict or provide early detection of the presence of a risk requiring a fast response," this project looks forward to benefiting from EWSs, particularly in terms of mitigating and responding to natural disasters (NATO, April 19, 2024).

Also launched in 2023, the multi-year project named "SAPIENCE: Sense & Avoid—a cooPeratIvE droNe CompEtition" brings together Austria, Netherlands, the UK, and the USA to explore the use of multi-agent Unmanned Aircraft Systems for management of civil emergencies. Likewise, France, Mauritania, and Romania united their forces in "PROMEDEUS: Protection Civile et Medecine d'Urgence Sanitaire en Mauritanie" to improve emergency medical assistance and treatment in the capital city of Nouakchott, Mauritania. This initiative also incorporates a medical care system in coordination with emergency services via telemedicine, thus helping trauma- and medical-emergency victims in and around Nouakchott. Featuring the first operational use of advanced technologies for medical response purposes, the project participants look forward to "establishing capabilities for alerts, emergency medical dispatching and operational coordination of response teams and pre-hospital emergency medicine throughout Mauritania" (NATO, April 19, 2024).

In 2024, NATO member states revised the list of thematic priorities for the SPS Program, to focus on "current and emerging security challenges that define NATO's strategic environment." They are alphabetically listed as follows. Beyond these 13 themes, any other proposal directly relevant to implementing NATO's core tasks is also eligible for SPS funding. Even though "Human and Social Aspects of Security" is featured as one of the themes, others in the list are complementary to this very priority (NATO, April 11, 2024):

· *Assessing and Addressing Threats Posed by the Russian Federation*
refers to the identifying methods and means to fight hybrid threats from this country, including hostile information activities.

· *Chemical, Biological, Radiological, and Nuclear (CBRN) and Explosive Hazards Management*
concerns with detecting Unexploded Ordnance (UXO) and undertaking "detection, decontamination, destruction, disposal, and containment of CBRN Agents," with a focus on recovery and countermeasures.

· *Counterterrorism*
relates to detecting and defending against terrorists' misuse of technology like improvised explosive devices and other illicit activities. It also involves Preventing/Countering Violent Extremism (P/CVE) to discourage people from joining the ranks of terrorist organizations.

· *Critical Underwater Infrastructure*
features technologies for detecting surface and underwater threats and monitoring and protecting related critical infrastructure.

· *Cyber Defense*
refers to technologies for available and confidential communication networks, situational awareness, and support to missions and operations.

· *Defense against Hybrid Threats*
covers technologies to "prepare, deter and defend against the coercive use of political, energy, information and other hybrid tactics by states and non-state actors." Its scope includes counter-disinformation by using AI tools to monitor, detect, and eliminate potential and actual malicious activities in online and offline contexts.

- *Energy Security*
  focuses on dual-use innovations in renewable energy, energy transition, and energy infrastructure security.
- *Environment, Climate Change and Security*
  calls for acknowledging and adapting to climate change-related environmental degradation and health issues in military missions and operations and seeks to mitigate the negative impact of military activities on the environment. Its agenda also covers forecasting and preventing natural disasters.
- *Human and Social Aspects of Security*
  refers to the cultural and social aspects of NATO's Human Security and WPS Agenda in missions and operations.
- *Innovation and Emerging Disruptive Technologies (EDTs)*
  explores the impact of malicious use of cutting-edge technologies on security like AI, biotechnologies, quantum, or space, and builds countermeasures for defense.
- *Operational Support*
  refers to civilian support for missions and operations, as well as benchmarking and promoting best practices in these activities.
- *Resilience*
  means strengthening civil preparedness in online and offline environments through inter-agency coordination mechanisms while protecting critical infrastructure, personnel, and supplies.
- *Strategic Foresight*
  highlights main global and regional defense and security trends for early warning and forecasting purposes.

It is against this background that on April 23–24, 2024, the NATO-Istanbul Cooperation Initiative (NATO-ICI) Regional Center based in Kuwait and the NATO Innovation, Hybrid and Cyber Division launched a second conference on the security implications of climate change. This occasion brought together experts and officials to brainstorm about the serious challenges encountered in the Middle East. Premised on the second Climate Change and Security Impact Assessment issued by NATO Secretary General Jens Stoltenberg last year, the conference underscored how NATO's southern neighborhood had been exponentially suffering from climate-related problems like "warmer temperatures on land and sea, rising sea levels and water scarcity" (NATO, April 24, 2024).

Another excellent example of NATO's technological collaboration with partners on subjects related to Human Security is Azerbaijan's time-honored involvement in NATO's SPS Program for missions like "neutralizing toxic rocket fuel left behind from Soviet times, securing energy infrastructure against seismic hazards, protecting cyber networks, and developing sensors for the detection of landmines and explosives" (NATO, September 27, 2024).

In October 2024, consecutive meetings were held in Bucharest, Romania (October 16) and Sofia, Bulgaria (October 22) to celebrate the decades-long security-related scientific contribution of both NATO members to the SPS Program. The SPS representatives visiting these countries announced the 2025 call for proposals to enable broader research and innovation based on new thematic priorities of the Program (NATO, October 16, 2024; NATO, October 22, 2024).

Evaluation and Conclusion

This chapter distinguishes between the use of technology for malicious ends and as a force for good. Focusing on the latter function, Peace Technology is a fresh discipline based on innovative approaches and tools to raise awareness about constructive means of conflict management, prevent conflicts, mitigate harm against civilians and critical infrastructure, and neutralize perpetrators in online and offline environments. Tackling traditional and non-traditional risks and threats in peacetime, crisis, and conflict scenarios, Peace Technology calls for cross-border networks of scientific communities to safeguard and render resilient civilian populations and properties. Today, national security is not equivalent to "Human Security," as states are increasingly sensitive or vulnerable to be able to offer a comprehensive safety net for their people against the tide of climate-induced food insecurity, trafficking in humans, arms, and drugs, or disinformation, among others. Peace Technology brings together officials and experts to produce hardware and software in the name of positive peace, in which people live without fear and need.

Even though the United Nations has the principal mandate for the betterment of people's lives, NATO has been investing in human security for member and partner populations for decades through scientific R&D. With the UN Charter constituting the backbone of the Alliance, NATO's traditional Cold War agenda has broadened to address challenges directly affecting civilians, property, infrastructure and environment both in times of peace and war. Peace Technology makes a difference in people's lives through capacity building, early warning, and post-conflict reconstruction activities. This attitude also reflects a gender-sensitive approach, demonstrative of NATO member and partner states' adherence to the word and spirit of the UN's Women, Peace and Security Agenda. In addition, NATO's ever-deepening Human Security perspective features a holistic approach in conformity with another UN Agenda on sustainability.

NATO's interest in Human Security also derives from its being a political alliance. Being mindful of human, societal, gender, and environmental dimensions of peace also distinguishes this organization from authoritarian state and non-state actors. Accordingly, even though scientific advancements under the NATO umbrella mainly serve operational interests, the Alliance is also attentive to peace technologies for human survival, dignity, and prosperity. Thus, NATO reaches out to like-minded partner states to exchange and implement ideas not only for "collective defense" but also "collective peace."

NATO's scientific and technological collaboration framework for peace and security relates to the Science for Peace and Security (SPS) Program launched in the early Cold War years. The Program centered on security-related civil science and technology to tackle emerging challenges and their spillover effect on international security. It underwent a comprehensive transformation in time, welcoming new stakeholders and engaging in cutting-edge R&D in the non-military field. Human Security features a large part of activities under the auspices of the SPS Program to serve its five pillars or cross-cutting topics, namely "Protection of Civilians (PoC); Protection of Children in Armed Conflict (CAAC); Combating Trafficking in Human Beings (CTHB); Conflict-related Sexual Violence (CRSV), and Cultural Property Protection (CPP)."

Although the SPS Program has yielded many fruitful outputs through multi-year projects and events like advanced research workshops and advanced training courses, some critics maintain that these have mainly focused on the protection of civilians but not, for example, fighting against trafficking, gender-based violence, or child abuse. Another criticism is about the carbon footprint of the NATO military-industrial complex, even though some products serve humanitarian responses (Birch, 2024, pp. 215–216). This argument is related to geopolitical conflicts, which fuel an escalating arms race, thus requiring high energy consumption to manufacture advanced technical tools and equipment and train the necessary military personnel to use them. The spread of militarized competition has serious economic consequences and paves the way for environmental devastation (Pata, Destek, Manga & Cengiz, 2023, pp. 1–2). This is evident in the "NATO's Defense Investment Pledge, under which member states have committed to spend at least 2% of GDP on defense" and devote "at least 20% of their defense expenditures to major new equipment spending, including the associated R&D." At the Washington Summit in July 2024, NATO accepted a new Industrial Capacity Expansion Pledge to bolster defense industrial joint work and enable member states to restock their arsenals as they deliver military assistance to Ukraine (NATO, July 15, 2024).

There is also debate about expanding the Human Security agenda and related technologies for NATO, concerning infectious diseases and pandemics. Even though NATO member states have taken several measures to respond collectively to the COVID-19 challenge, critics argue that these efforts should not be *ad hoc* and temporary. Notwithstanding the World Health Organization's (WHO) extensive amendments to its International Health Regulations in 2024, and despite the increased cross-border solidarity of states, NGOs, and companies under the Global Health Security Agenda, the active engagement of military organizations is missing. Such organizations are more competent to undertake global health-related missions with speed, discipline, and greater efficiency. For NATO's part, this kind of engagement would be entirely consistent with the spirit of its founding charter, especially when other more relevant actors like the WHO become incapacitated by discord, competition, and polarization in world affairs (Seifman, July 16, 2024).

As conclusion, the Alliance's efforts to harness science and technology in the name of peace and human security should be commended. On the other hand, NATO would serve humanity more appropriately if the scope of "peace technologies" is extended to cover and go beyond all the five elements of its human security agenda. Finally, regardless of how geopolitical contests and hybrid challenges in current times call for increases in defense expenditures, NATO should balance its plans, funding, and production for both military and civilian resilience.

Classifying New Nationalism: Shifting Perceptions of Adversaries in Globalized East and West

Günce Sabah Eryılmaz

Introduction

The concept of "new nationalism" is understood as a manifestation of nationalism within a contemporary global and transnational milieu. It represents novel forms of interaction with and responses to recent economic, political, and socio-cultural developments, including globalization, regionalization, multiculturalism, and migration (Gingrich & Banks, 2006, s. 2–7). New nationalist attitudes, narratives and actions are often closely linked to certain narrow political ideologies or positions, such as nativism, far-right populism, cultural separatism, anti-establishment, anti-globalization, anti-immigration, protectionism, xenophobia and Euroscepticism (Mudde, 1999; Ignazi, 2003; Bergmann, 2020).

The tenets of the new nationalism are believed to be founded upon "ethnocentrism," a concept that has evolved to become considerably more nuanced than the overt racism that was prevalent during the first half of the twentieth century. In accordance with these tenets, "culture" is posited as the contemporary equivalent of "race." New nationalist groups place a particular emphasis on the promotion of their own national values, history, and traditions. In this way, they seek to establish a tangible and conceptual demarcation between their own nation and those of other countries (Horáková, 2019, s. 128). However, this demarcation is not merely physical and mental. New nationalist ideologies also construct an emotional barrier that serves to reinforce the distinction between "us" and "the other" (Koschut, 2018a) by mobilizing sentiments of insecurity (Gingrich & Banks, 2006), fear, anger, and victimization (Bithymitris, 2017; Horáková, 2019) within society.

While New nationalism has recently gained significant attention as a research subject, its definition and historical background remain contentious. Numerous new nationalist ideologies exist in the vast literature, yet a universally accepted classification is lacking. The absence of a clear categorization hampers effective comparative analysis and limits our ability to systematically study the varied manifestations of new nationalism. This chapter seeks to address this gap by proposing a structured classification of new nationalisms, emphasizing key distinctions among them. By doing so, it aims to enhance the clarity and comparability of research in this field, providing scholars with a more robust analytical tool to navigate and understand the increasingly complex landscape of new nationalism.

The Evolution and Context of New Nationalisms

In the period following the Cold War, there has been a notable increase in the prevalence of nationalist sentiment. In particular, the nationalist parties[1] that achieved electoral success or gained the ability to influence the political agenda during and after the 1990s are the subject of study by researchers who have identified various forms of these parties, including right-populism, nationalist-populism, nativist-populism, far-right, radical-right, and so forth.

The categorization of emerging nationalist parties and movements as either right-wing or left-wing is a pervasive phenomenon in political science (Harrison & Bruter, 2011; Mudde, 1999; Golder, 2003). While these categorizations offer a degree of explanatory power, they have limitations. Economic policies, which are an essential determinant of the left-right ideological axis, have been transforming. To illustrate, the distinction between liberal economic policies based on capital mobility and redistributive welfare state

---

[1] The main parties in Europe and their foundation years can be listed as follows: Austrian Freedom Party (Austria-1956), National Democratic Party (Germany-1964), National Front (National Unity) (France-1967), Swiss People's Party (Switzerland-1971), Progress Party (Norway-1973), British National Party (United Kingdom-1982), Republicans (Germany-1983), Golden Dawn (Greece-1985), Sweden Democrats (Sweden-1988), Fidesz (Hungary-1990), Northern League (Italy-1991), Hungarian Justice and Life Party (Hungary-1993), UK Independence Party (UK-1993), Danish People's Party (Denmark-1995), True Finns (Finland-1995), Orthodox People's Revival (Greece-2000), National Renewal Party (Portugal-2000), Flemish Importance (Belgium-2004), Union for the Future of Austria (Austria-2005), Freedom Party (Netherlands-2006), etc. Mounk ve Kyle (2018) find that 46 populist leaders have come to power in 33 democratic countries since the 1990s. Some of them are leaders of the above-mentioned parties.

and transnational developments, it is also inherently country-specific, shaped by the legacy of traditional nationalism and the historical circumstances of the nation or region in question. To illustrate, the new nationalism in Western Europe is inextricably linked to the colonial legacy of these countries. Meanwhile, the new nationalism in Turkey is shaped by the enduring impact of the Ottoman Empire's dissolution, which continues to leave an indelible mark on the collective psyche.

The advent of new nationalism is dated by scholars according to a variety of chronological frameworks. Bergman (2020, s. 26–27) argues that new nationalist sentiments and movements arose in three waves after the 1950s. He dates the emergence of new nationalism to a relatively earlier period. This approach posits that the initial phase of new nationalism emerged just before the 1970 oil crisis, manifesting as nationalist movements and far-right parties in European states, including France, Denmark, and Norway. These movements were driven by opposition to significant tax burdens and multiculturalism. The second wave of new nationalism was triggered by the arrival of Eastern European migrant workers in Western Europe following the fall of the Berlin Wall in 1989. The most recent wave commenced in the wake of the 2008 global financial crisis and has exerted a considerable influence on the political landscape of Europe, reaching its zenith in recent years.[3] As previously mentioned at the outset of this chapter, other scholars have dated the emergence of new nationalism to the 1990s (Gingrich & Banks, 2006; Duroy, 2020; Winichakul, 2008; Kersten, 1999; Van der Wende, 2020). The most significant factor contributing to this determination is the enhanced capacity of new nationalisms to disseminate to broader populations and establish the political agenda. In the 1990s, as the effects of globalization intensified, new nationalist ideologies were able to flourish in several contexts.

Defining "New" in New Nationalisms

The concept of new nationalism is fundamentally based on the existence of old nationalism, characterized by a certain continuity due to its nature

---

[3] In his analysis of the relationship between crises and nationalism, Wang (2021, s. 20), refers to Bergman's chronology, emphasizing that the relationship is not linear or unidirectional.

as nationalism. Both classical and new nationalism are deeply intertwined with the capitalist system and the structure of the state. Classical nationalism emerged during the early stages of capitalism, while new nationalism has developed in the late capitalist era, within the context of evolving capitalist relations (Gingrich, 2006, s. 198–199). This evolution underscores the dynamism of the field and the need for continuous research and analysis.

Despite these commonalities, new nationalism differs from classical nationalism in several ways. New nationalist movements often operate through parliamentary channels and utilize local cultures as a basis to mobilize people against perceived threats. While older nationalisms were often organized around race, the discourse of new nationalism focuses on cultural fundamentalism (Duroy, 2020, s. 13; Gingrich & Banks, 2006, s. 15; Horáková, 2019, s. 128). The new form of nationalism has a three-part hierarchical ideological platform. At the center is a coherent, culturally essentialist "us," positioned against two groups. The first group, the "they," is above "us" in power. Examples of this group include the EU authority and its mysterious collaborators. The second "them" is below "us" in power. This group includes local migrants and other cultural and linguistic minorities, as well as their dangerous collaborators in Asia and Africa (Gingrich, 2006, s. 199). According to Scheiring's research on the Hungarian working class, there are additional complexities, particularly about the "them" above. In the interviews, workers identify various elites as "they above," including transnational capital, liberal elites, and corrupt politicians (Scheiring, 2020, s. 1172–1173). Similarly, in examining the research conducted by Bithymitris (2017) on workers in Greece, it is observed that the "they" encompasses a multitude of nuances. Through critical discourse analysis, Bithymitris posits that socio-cultural and emotional factors shape workers' adoption of the new nationalism.

Another defining feature of the contemporary phenomenon of nationalism is its populist character. As previously discussed, a group of scholars has designated these new nationalist movements as "national/right-wing populism" (Mudde, 1999; Brubaker, 2017b; Rodrik, 2021). The ideology of populism constructs politics and determines its discourses based on the distinction between "the people" and "the elites." The group it characterizes as the people is positioned against an economic, political, and cultural elite group (Mudde, 2004). In this context, the people are regarded as morally upright, experiencing economic challenges, hardworking, attached to their families, outspoken, sincere, and guided by common sense, whereas the elites are viewed as rich, powerful, well-connected, (over)educated, and in control of institutions. The perception is that elites inhabit a distinct realm, subject to disparate norms and free from the constraints of economic hardship. They are assumed to prioritize their own interests and are frequently regarded as corrupt. Consequently, they are perceived as incapable of comprehending the issues and concerns of the public. They constantly look down on the values, habits and ways of life of ordinary people (Brubaker, 2017a, s. 363).

The study of populism frequently concentrates on the vertical hierarchy, but less so on the horizontal distinction. In particular, the advent of new nationalist ideologies has underscored the significance of the horizontal distinction, or the differentiation within the people, as a pivotal element of these new nationalist ideologies. In light of the public's conceptualization as a collective entity with defined boundaries, the distinction that emerges horizontally is that between "insiders" and "outsiders." Right-populism delineates the boundaries of collectivity in ethnic and cultural terms, characterizing those groups or forces that it perceives as threatening its shared and distinctive way of life as outsiders. In some instances, these outsiders may also be "outsiders within us," that is, citizens of the same state who are not considered to belong to the "people" (Brubaker, 2017a, s. 363). At this juncture, populist discourse in each country may diverge based on the historical conditions of that country, the symbols utilized in politics, and the representations and narratives about the groups within the country (Jansen, 2011, s. 84). In some countries, immigrants (even if they have acquired citizenship) are excluded from the collective identity, while in others, ethnic minorities or groups with different skin colors who are perceived to be in collaboration with the elites are excluded.

A further distinction between new and old nationalism is the social composition of their supporters. While the unemployed and endangered farmers have been prominent among new nationalist supporters, urbanites with jobs have also been significant constituencies. These are not those who have been most adversely affected by globalization but those who perceive a loss of privilege because of it (Gingrich, 2006, s. 199). They are those who fear a downward social mobilization. This fear is based on the perception that they will lose status in the future. When this loss of status occurs and the "other" is seen as the cause of this loss, their feelings turn into anger and rage (Kemper T., 2001, s. 66; Mann & Fenton, 2017, s. 7–8). This emotional state then motivates these groups to align with new nationalist ideologies. Consequently, contrary to popular belief, individuals espousing these ideologies are, in fact, those who have attained a certain status. However, they perceive that they will lose or have already lost this status.

Bieber (2018, s. 537) raises the question of whether nationalism is on the rise. He argues that there is no single general trend, but rather that nationalist policies, parties, and discourses are on the rise in some countries. He then examines the reasons for this rise and makes a similar observation to the fear of downward social mobilization. The sense of "insecurity" caused by globalization, especially as economic globalization has increased the uncertainty between people at the local level, reinforces status anxiety, while at the same time combining with other fears in the cultural sphere. The migrant crisis and multiculturalism policies have also led to concerns that cultural identity may be at risk. These insecurities, worries, and fears provide the necessary environment for the emergence of new nationalist movements (Gingrich & Banks, 2006, s. 14–16).

Lastly, while the old nationalism was somehow related to colonialism, the new nationalism is characterized by a strategy of isolation and closure rather than expansionism in the postcolonial period. Especially the desire to build a "Fortress Europe" is an example of this. "Fortress Europe" aims to keep out immigrants and threats from abroad, as well as agricultural products from Africa and Asia. In this way, they want to use it as a competitive tool against their global economic rivals America and Japan (Gingrich, 2006, s. 199). In this context, new nationalism is becoming an important oppositional ideology against neoliberal globalization and its strong opening-up policies in many European countries (Joppke, 2021, s. 87). These discussions are interrelated with those concerning the nation-state and borders. The new nationalist movements are situated within the confines of established nation-states. In contrast to the old nationalism, which sought to align the boundaries of the nation with those of the governing unit, the new nationalism typically emerges within borders that are recognized as both national (internal) and international (external) (Eger & Valdez, 2014, s. 13).

Gingrich and Banks (2006, s. 17) posit that the resurgence of nationalism cannot be equated with the re-emergence of the fascist regimes of Hitler, Franco, and Mussolini. The contemporary manifestations of new nationalisms employ these elements and symbols as instruments, yet their objectives are wholly situated within the present. To gain a deeper comprehension of the nature of new nationalism, it is frequently deemed beneficial to place emphasis on its position in the context of globalization. However, this should not be considered a direct consequence of globalization. In this way, new nationalism can be regarded as a movement that is in opposition to the current stage of globalization and is in competition with other anti-globalization and alternative globalization movements. In this regard, new nationalisms have become sufficiently influential to compel political parties in the center to prioritize the policies and discourses of new nationalist parties and movements in order to retain their voter base (Van der Wende, 2020, s. 3; Scheiring, 2020, s. 1160). In addition to their antagonistic relationship with globalization, new nationalist ideologies also position themselves against a range of other ideas, groups, and institutions, including liberal democracy, multiculturalism, transnational organizations, international economic and political cooperation, and immigrants. Consequently, when considering new nationalism, it is essential to take all these processes and relations into account collectively rather than acting from a narrow, single-focused perspective.

Classifying New Nationalisms: A Two-Pronged Approach

Despite the inherent challenges in making sweeping generalizations about the phenomenon of new nationalism, a classification system can be proposed, provided that the nuances and distinctions between the various forms of new nationalism are acknowledged and respected. New nationalism arises within the context of a prevailing international system characterized by the dominance of nation-states. As previously stated, nationalism is inextricably linked to the nation-state (Breuilly, 2005). Accordingly, new nationalism can be classified by its relationship with the nation-state. The first category is that of new nationalist ideology, which challenges the authority of the nation-state and calls for secession or autonomy from it. This form of nationalism is often referred to as separatist new nationalism. The second category is defensive new nationalism, which aims to reinforce and preserve the nation-state from perceived threats. In this regard, Berezin's (2002) conceptualization of the secure state provides a valuable framework for elucidating this distinction. Separatist new nationalism emerges when the nation-state fails to provide security for its own group. Defensive new nationalism, on the other hand, is nationalism based on the perception of a constant threat to the current form of the state in which a group lives, while accepting its nostalgic form and old system of values as a secure state.

This classification is reminiscent of the traditional typology of nationalism. However, there are fundamental differences. For example, the nationalists of the nineteenth century sought to disassociate themselves from the empires and their institutions and elites, to establish their nation-states. In the contemporary era, empires have ceased to exist as political entities. The new separatist nationalism is now engaged in a struggle with the nation-state. Consequently, both political institutions are distinct, and the economic structure is entirely disparate. While the old nationalism sought to challenge mercantilism and establish a capitalist market economy within their respective nation-states (Carr, 1945, s. 3–6), the new nationalism emerges at a time when capitalism has become the dominant mode of production, undergoing a transformation in response to global changes. Similarly, it would be accurate to categorize the non-separatist nationalisms of the nineteenth century as "founding nationalism." The objective of founding nationalism was to transform absolutist empires into nation-states. The new defensive nationalism does not seek to transform the nation-state in which it is formed. Conversely, it strives to preserve the nation-state against the effects of globalization, migration, and multiculturalism.

Separatist New Nationalism

Prominent figures in the literature on nationalism tend to view separatist "old" nationalisms with skepticism. Although they adopt disparate approaches to this form of nationalism, which originated in the developed Western world, they all consider this form within the broader context of nationalism (Hobsbawm E. J., 1999, s. 257; Hobsbawm & Kertzer, 1992; Smith A. D., 2004, s. 213–218). Given that separatist "old" nationalisms are themselves a topic of contention in the field of nationalism studies and are sometimes even characterized as "new" in contrast to traditional founding nationalism, the question of what is "new" in separatist new nationalism remains a matter of debate.

The recent developments in the field of new nationalism literature have witnessed a shift in focus from separatist new nationalisms to defensive new nationalisms (Bithymitris, 2017; Bergmann, 2020; Bangstad, 2015; Horáková, 2019). Nevertheless, separatist new nationalism is also included to a certain extent in the field of new nationalism studies. For example, Zhou (2022) references separatist new nationalism as one of the new types of nationalism in his study on the characteristics and trends of new nationalism in the twenty-first century. In a similar vein to other authors in this field, he examines new nationalisms in developed countries. Since separatist new nationalisms in these countries can preserve their political and cultural autonomy due to democratic governments, they are mostly driven by economic motives. Zhou argues that what distinguishes these nationalisms from the old version is economic egoism and chauvinism. He cites Scottish nationalism in England, Catalan nationalism in Spain, and Flemish nationalism in Belgium as examples (Zhou, 2022, s. 6–7).[4] Quebec nationalism in Canada can also be added to these nationalisms. DeCosta (1995, s. 295–6) states that the separatist old nationalism in Quebec was shaped through the discourse of anti-colonialism. The new nationalism, on the other hand, raises economic and social issues and emphasizes the diversity of Quebec society.

As McCrone (2002) notes, separatist new nationalism is emerging in the wealthier parts of developed countries. He examines this nationalism and its relationship to economic interests through three case studies: Scotland, Catalonia, and Quebec. The emergence of separatist new nationalism in Quebec coincides with the development of a neoliberal economic approach and the advent of a new market following the signing of the North American Free Trade Agreement (NAFTA). The region of Catalonia is already a wealthy area of Spain. While trade relations have been interrupted at times, they have been on the rise again after Franco. Research on the Catalan separatist movement suggests that taxation and other fiscal policies, rather than cultural reasons, have influenced the idea of separatism (Boylan, 2015). In Scotland, oil reserves in the north combine economic and nationalist demands (McCrone, 2002).

The phenomenon of separatist new nationalism has often emerged in contexts where globalization, shifts in economic conditions, and the formation of supranational and regional cooperation have created a favorable

---

4   Zhou (2022) identifies four types of new nationalism: far-right nationalism, evangelical nationalism, separatist nationalism, and Third World religious nationalism.

environment for its proliferation. As Beaudet (1993, s. 2648) posits, the crisis of the nation-state in the context of globalization represents a primary catalyst for the resurgence of separatist new nationalist ideologies. In the wake of the global crisis, groups that have formed their own communities (linguistic, religious, ethnic) have increasingly demanded secession from the nation-state. At this juncture, the new nationalist ideology serves as a unifying force for these groups. The advent of separatist new nationalisms is included in Bergmann's periodization as part of the initial wave of new nationalisms that emerged in the wake of the 1970 Oil Crisis (Bergmann, 2020). To explain this, Hearn (2002, s. 19) employs a Weberian analysis of the shifts in class positions and alliances between classes in Scotland, examining the relationship between status groups and civil society. This analysis posits that the welfare state practices that emerged in the wake of the First World War served to empower the class of urban professionals further, facilitating their ascension to managerial positions. While the Conservative Party was unable to align its ideology with these classes, the Labor Party and the Scottish National Party were able to do so. This "new class" provided support for the Keynesian project and socialist states in the West and East during the mid-twentieth century. However, the crisis of the welfare state in the 1970s led the last generation of the new class to reconsider their social role. The Scottish demands for autonomy and/or independence can be seen as an outcome of this process (Hearn, 2002, s. 22). Hearn's explanation of the separatist new nationalism is based on the nationalist "new class." This foundation provides an appropriate starting point for including the impact of globalization and the economic interests of the actors in the analysis.

Globalization has not only resulted in alterations to economic policies but has also facilitated the emergence of new supranational and transnational institutions and organizations. A regional organization such as the European Union (EU) is primarily concerned with the integration of its constituent regions. Nevertheless, while this approach to integration is effective at the international level, it can also result in the emergence of secessionist movements within nation-states. In his analysis of separatist new nationalism in Scotland, Stéphane Paquin (2007, s. 55–56) posits that the forces of globalization and European integration have eroded the authority of the nation-state, thereby fostering a phenomenon of intra-national disintegration. He argues that the most significant factor contributing to the emergence of this situation is "*paradiplomacy.*" The phenomenon of *paradiplomacy* arises when, because of globalization, the nation-state loses its monopoly of representation in the international arena. Consequently, subnational nationalist movements can engage in diplomatic activities at the international level. Through *paradiplomacy*, Scottish political elites can bypass the United Kingdom diplomatic apparatus and communicate directly with EU institutions and diplomats, thereby setting their own agenda.[5]

It would be inaccurate to suggest that the EU's influence on regional separatist groups and their separatist new nationalism can be represented by a single, unified line. As previously stated, the evolution of the EU during the 1990s and early 2000s reinforced separatist new nationalisms due to the simultaneous decline in the authority of nation-states and the devolution of powers, coupled with the increased visibility and representation of autonomous regional governments in the international arena through methods such as *paradiplomacy.* Conversely, because of the impact of EU policies, separatist new nationalists are acquiring greater cultural and economic autonomy, representing their own national interests with greater frequency in political decision-making processes, and there is a reduction in their demands for independence (Saylan, 2011). A comparable process can be observed in Quebec nationalism. Since the mid-2000s, there has been a notable increase in stable cooperation between the federal government and the Quebec government, which has experienced economic growth following the implementation of NAFTA, and demands for independence have declined (Changfoot & Cullen, 2011). While demands for full independence may be waning, separatist groups

---

[5] The argument that EU integration strengthens separatist new nationalisms is incomplete without consideration of the following aspect. Furthermore, it serves to reinforce the stance of new nationalisms that seek to incorporate populations beyond the confines of their own territories. For example, during and after the EU accession process, new nationalist parties in Hungary have advanced the claim of annexing territories inhabited by Hungarians outside its borders to Hungary. Despite the absence of a change in borders and an expansion of Hungary's territory, the EU membership of neighboring countries enabled these countries to act more effectively within their respective ethnic spheres of influence. The Hungarian government developed special practices for Hungarians living in neighboring countries. These practices were also in line with the EU's decentralization project. Therefore, it can be said that the new nationalist ruling party achieved the reunification it had dreamed of to a certain extent (Fox & Vermeersch, 2010, s. 331; Minkenberg & Perrineau, 2007, s. 43–44).

are simultaneously experiencing an increase in nationalist sentiments, a stronger emphasis on safeguarding their national economic interests, and an enhanced capacity for autonomous political maneuvering.

The study of separatist new nationalism is less prevalent in the field of new nationalism research than the study of defensive new nationalism. These nationalisms are either studied directly under the rubric of separatism and regionalism. Most of the existing literature is devoted to the study of defensive new nationalism. Nevertheless, in the forthcoming period—particularly as defensive new nationalisms intensify—separatist new nationalisms will likewise gain momentum and prominence. An illustrative example of this phenomenon can be observed in the emergence of independence-related demands in Scotland following the United Kingdom's withdrawal from the European Union. Because of the rise in defensive new nationalism in the UK and its anti-EU populist discourse, the country exited the EU. The Scots, who strongly opposed this process, subsequently adopted an increasingly independent position after Brexit referendum (McEwen, 2018). Therefore, it is important not to neglect the ongoing interaction between these two types of new nationalism.

Defensive New Nationalism: Protectionist Responses to Globalization

Defensive new nationalism does not entail a demand for separation and/ or autonomy from the nation-state in which it is situated. Adherents of this nationalist ideology perceive themselves as the founding element and primary guardian of the nation-state in which they reside. In this context, defensive new nationalism shares similarities with the nationalist ideologies that emerged during the process of nation-state formation. These ideologies aim to reform the state. Prominent actors within the new nationalist ideology frequently reference the foundational processes of nations, and at times present themselves as the continuation of this endeavor (Laruelle, 2009, s. 155; Kenez, 1992, s. 2; Hellström & Nilsson, 2008, s. 9). The embrace of a successful nation-state model can be seen as a strategy that will enable defensive new nationalism to gain broader acceptance.

To illustrate, a comparison of traditional and contemporary Chinese nationalism reveals that the former manifested in a distinct set of characteristics during the 1910s. Wu (2008) enumerates these as follows: The primary factors that shaped the emergence of traditional nationalism were economic deprivation and underdevelopment. The Chinese population experienced feelings of humiliation in the context of their interactions with Western powers and consequently developed a sense of urgency to "save China." The issues of political corruption and the shortcomings of Confucianism are perceived as problematic. The primary focus of traditional nationalism is not the concept of a nation as a distinct entity. They believe that acquiring resources from the West will result in economic and political advancement for the Chinese nation. This form of nationalism can be described as rational, progressive, and developmental. The new nationalism of the 1990s is distinguished from the preceding form by its focus on China's economic achievements. The primary question currently at the forefront is not how to save China, but rather, how to position China as a global leader, if it is not already. This economic success is giving rise to a reassessment of official Chinese nationalism in the political and cultural spheres. There is a renewed focus on China's cultural resources as a source of legitimacy. This is a cultural, conservative, and identity-centered nationalism that employs a statist approach. It supports China's authoritarian communist regime and is characterized by an embrace of Confucian doctrine and affirmation of other Chinese traditions. This has led to the emergence of cultural chauvinism (Wu, 2008, s. 478–479). An additional case study for differentiating between traditional and defensive new nationalism can be observed in Japan. Kersten identifies the historical emergence of old nationalism in Japan as a form that preceded and coincided with the war. This form of nationalism was characterized by a top-down approach, loyalty to the emperor, and a perception of the state as a "family state." In contrast, the new nationalism strives to establish autonomy between the nation and the state. It also aims to rehabilitate the form of nationalism that has been constrained by post-war democracy (Kersten, 1999, s. 193).

The aim of defensive new nationalism is to protect the nation-state against the "other," which they perceive as a threat, and to make it stronger. A substantial body of research on nationalist ideology underscores the pivotal role of the "us versus them" dichotomy in the formation of national identity. Nationalism constructs the notion of "I" as part of a collective "We," integrating everyone into a larger community. The national identity of "We" is established through its relationship with the "Other." Consequently, nationalism not only constructs the "We" but also defines the "Other." This process of defining the "Other" allows nationalism to highlight the distinctiveness of the national identity it creates. In this way, the boundaries of this identity are delineated (DeCoste, 1995, s. 309–310). The defensive form of new nationalism assumes the existence of an "other" that cannot be incorporated into the nation. This other is regarded as an adversary and perceived as a threat. The objective is to protect and reinforce the nation and the nation-state against this perceived threat. This threat may emerge from within the nation as an internal threat or from external sources.

Defensive New Nationalism Against Internal "Others"

Defensive new nationalisms, which are oriented in opposition to the other within the nation-state, are typically observed in developed Western countries. The primary catalyst for the advent of this form of nationalism in Western European countries is the influx of immigrants resulting from their economic advancement and enhanced quality of life. This immigration has two significant consequences. Initially, the influx was so rapid and intense that it was not feasible to integrate new immigrants into society. Secondly, the influx of new immigrants has resulted in a diminishing of the social welfare available to the lower classes. As a result, these social groups perceive immigrants as a threat (Castels, 2005, s. 305).

This type of defensive new nationalism views the "other" within the nation-state as immigrants and shapes its policies accordingly. At this juncture, quantitative studies on new nationalist parties in Europe concentrate on examining the correlation between their votes and migration, unemployment, and economic conditions (Golder, 2003, s. 433; Harrison & Bruter, 2011, s. 13). Golder (2003, s. 460) argues that the impact of unemployment on the electoral support of far-right populist parties is contingent. The presence of a significant immigrant population in a country can influence electoral outcomes. It is a common observation that high immigration rates facilitate the growth of far-right populist parties, leading to an increase in their electoral support. The level of unemployment is an insufficient indicator. In a similar vein, Ivarsflaten's research into elections in seven Western European countries (Austria, Denmark, Flanders, France, the Netherlands, Norway, and Switzerland) around 2002 yielded comparable results. In these elections, no party that did not address immigration achieved electoral success. Conversely, right-wing parties that addressed immigration achieved electoral success, even in the absence of addressing economic issues, the problem of elitism and corruption in politics (Ivarsflaten, 2008, s. 15–17).

Nevertheless, the introduction of migration issues does not invariably result in the reinforcement of defensive new nationalist parties in all countries. Macroeconomic conditions (such as unemployment) and differences in national culture (for example, whether a culture is individualistic or not) can lead to differences in the perception of migrants as a threat (Davis & Deole, 2017, s. 14). For example, as evidenced by Swank and Betz's study (2003, s. 239), immigration rates have been observed to correlate with an increase in votes for right-wing populist parties. However, it is important to note that this observed phenomenon is contingent upon the specific welfare state practices in place within a given country. The impact of immigration on voting patterns diminishes when welfare state practices are robust. In conclusion, while anti-immigrant sentiment represents a central tenet of defensive new nationalism, the extent to which these parties will gain support is influenced by macroeconomic and cultural conditions within the country in question. When analyzing these parties, it is essential to consider the ideology of defensive new nationalism on the supply side and the conditions that contribute to the formation of the demand side together (Golder, 2016, s. 490–491).

Moreover, it is important to consider Mudde's argument in this context. It is inaccurate to describe far-right parties as single-issue parties. Migration is neither the sole issue nor the most pivotal one. The issue of migration plays a functional role in achieving electoral success. It is an issue that links xenophobic nationalism, which represents the ideological center of far-right parties, with the growing unrest in society and even resentment among voters (Mudde, 1999, s. 192). Other salient issues that far-right parties frequently highlight include anti-political sentiment, the role of the welfare state, and law and order. Nationalism constitutes an essential element of their ideological framework (Mudde, 1999, s. 193). In his later works, Mudde (2015, s. 296) identifies nativism, a combination of nationalism and xenophobia, as a key characteristic of populist radical right parties. He asserts that this ideological stance serves to differentiate between the native group, defined as the "nation," and the nonnative group, defined as the "alien." Consequently, the latter group is excluded from the nation.

Defensive new nationalism against internal threats can be defined by two main characteristics. Firstly, this type of new nationalism arises from a crisis of national identity. As a result of the transnationalism that has arisen because of globalization, the national identities that are prevalent in Europe are becoming increasingly ambiguous (Hellström & Nilsson, 2008, p. 2). The influx of migrants, particularly during the 1990s, represents another significant factor contributing to this crisis. In its most fundamental sense, nationalism establishes a connection between the cultural entity, the nation, and the political entity, the state. Its success in the modern period is dependent on this factor (Schwarzmantel, 2008, s. 92). Nationalism is characterized by two co-existing and competing dimensions: solidarity and otherness. The establishment of national identity gives rise to a sense of solidarity among the citizens who collectively constitute the nation. Conversely, those who are not part of the nation are regarded as "others," and are consequently excluded from the horizontal equality and solidarity that characterizes the national community. It is crucial to identify the factors that differentiate us from them. The impact of migration has the effect of preventing the completion of this dual axis. As a potential solution to this problem, the new nationalist ideology seeks to redefine national identity in a more essentialist manner. The objective of the new nationalism is to exclude individuals who do not align with the "original" ethos of the state and the nation, thereby reducing the discrepancy caused by the structural incompatibility between nationality and citizenship (Duroy, s. 14–15; Schwarzmantel, 2008, s. 99). Those who are deemed a threat to the social order and national security are often immigrants, perceived as posing a potential danger within the nation. In this manner, the new nationalist ideology signifies a redefinition of borders and the separation of the nation from the external world, thereby reducing the fear of incompleteness (Hellström & Nilsson, 2008, s. 2). As a result, all actors have avoided engaging with the racial discourse that was characteristic of older forms of nationalism and fascism. Instead of racial discourse, the new nationalist ideology employs the concept of culture. This precludes the possibility of being accused of racism for advocating a homogeneous monoculture (Hellström & Nilsson, 2008, s. 21; Bangstad, 2015, s. 51; Hervik, 2011, s. 33–36).

Brubaker (2017b) posits that defensive new nationalism (what he terms "national populism") against internal threats constitutes a novel cluster with distinctive characteristics in Northern and Western Europe. The new nationalist ideologies that have emerged in this region interpret the distinction between "us" and "the other" in terms of civilizationism, rather than defining it in narrow terms based on ethnic, essentialist national identity. As a result, these nationalisms perceive Islam as the primary source of threat to civilization, leading to the development of a counter stance through the themes of Christianity, secularism, and liberalism. These ideologies simultaneously highlight the perceived threat that Islam poses to civilization while also recognizing Christianity as a cultural and civilizational identity. As they become increasingly preoccupied with the public display of Muslim symbols and practices, they highlight the secular nature of their own identity. While they oppose the perceived threat of "Islamization" to Jewish, female, homosexual, and free-expression rights, they express their commitment to gender equality, gay rights, and free expression through liberal discourse (Brubaker, Between nationalism and civilizationism: The European populist moment in comparative perspective, 2017b, s. 1197–1198). In these nationalisms, civilizationalism can be understood as a form of nationalism, a mode of discourse about the "nation" that is constituted by the civilizational language used to define the content of national culture and national identity (Brubaker, 2017b, s. 1211).

Secondly, a sense of insecurity is one of the most fundamental emotions associated with a defensive new nationalism. This sentiment can be attributed to two primary factors: the apprehension regarding the incompleteness of national identity and the advent of novel risks associated with globalization. In particular, the erosion of welfare state practices by neoliberal economic policies is contributing to a situation in which the security of life and the ability to predict the future are becoming increasingly problematic. The collapse of the welfare state in economic life and the influx of migrants from disparate cultural backgrounds have introduced a climate of uncertainty. Furthermore, the constant criminalization of migrants due to their association with crime serves to heighten the perception of threat. To illustrate this point, one may consider the Sweden Democrats (Sverigedemokraterna-SD), a defensive new nationalist party in Sweden, which has positioned itself against globalization, neoliberalism, and internationalization. From an economic standpoint, they identify as genuine social democrats and advocate for the continued implementation of welfare state policies. They regard immigration as Sweden's defining historical phenomenon and are dedicated to establishing Sweden as a nation for Swedes alone (Hellström & Nilsson, 2008, s. 9–11). These policies collectively aim to address feelings of insecurity. In situations of perceived insecurity, individuals may tend to withdraw from potentially threatening situations and seek protection. Furthermore, Alden and Schurmann (1992, s. 106–108) identify protectionist policies in the early stages of new nationalism in the United States. In this context, the new nationalism adopted an isolationist stance, advocating for support and regulation of the economy and the strengthening of infrastructure. These isolationist policies have intensified during the Trump era, leading to a notable distance not only economically but also in terms of international cooperation and organizations (Haynes, 2021).

In conclusion, while defensive new nationalism in Western countries often emerges as a response to perceived internal threats, it is important to recognize that this form of nationalism can also incorporate elements of external threats. The perception of both internal and external threats within defensive new nationalism is not mutually exclusive; rather, they can and often do coexist. For example, nationalist movements in Europe that are primarily focused on countering internal threats may also adopt a stance against the EU, which is perceived as an external threat (Down & Han, 2021). However, in the development of these new nationalist ideologies, the internal threat and its polarizing effects tend to be the primary focus, with the external threat, such as the EU, serving as a complementary or reinforcing factor.

Defensive New Nationalism Against External Threats

The instances where the threat perception of defensive new nationalism is directed toward external entities are more commonly observed in countries of the Global South or non-Western regions. While this form of nationalism shares core characteristics with defensive nationalism that targets internal threats, the nature of the external threat leads to variations in focus and emphasis.

This form of defensive new nationalism is also positioned in opposition to the processes of globalization and neoliberal policies. Nevertheless, this opposition is not solely a consequence of the detrimental consequences of these policies; it also serves to differentiate between the self and the other. Globalization and neoliberal policies are perceived as neocolonial policies in countries that were formerly colonized (Banerjee, 2005, s. 3629; Winichakul,

2008, s. 586). At this juncture, these policies influence the development of nationalism within the country. The immigrants themselves are not perceived as the "other"; rather, the focus is on the imperial West. Winichakul's study of Thai nationalism reveals that a new form of nationalism, constructed by former leftists and intellectuals, has gained traction following the 1997 economic crisis and the advent of globalization. This emerging nationalism is deeply rooted in anti-Western sentiment. In the case of Thai nationalism, the West consistently serves as the "other," yet this relationship is inherently paradoxical: while the West is simultaneously seen as an aspirational model, it is also viewed as a potential threat (Callahan, 2003, s. 496; Winichakul, 2008, s. 585–586; Eaksittipong, 2021, s. 104–106).

In countries that entered the modernization process at a later stage, Western modernization is frequently perceived through a dualistic lens, encompassing both aspiration and apprehension. This duality frequently gives rise to feelings of *ressentiment* (Greenfeld, 1994). From this perspective, it is unsurprising that the new nationalism in Thailand is embraced by segments of society that are Westernized, consumerist, materialistic, and even capitalist (Winichakul, 2008, s. 586). This is because these groups are the ones who feel the strongest desire for the West, who attempt to imitate it, but are the most disappointed when they realize that they are unable to succeed in this imitation due to the structural conditions present in their own countries. These groups then begin to emphasize their authenticity through a historical and cultural heritage in society. Indeed, Winichakul (2008, s. 582) states that the primary objective of Chatthip who pioneered the new nationalism in Thailand, was to search for the authentic *Thai* people and to define them through language and cultural commonality.

The identity crisis that defensive new nationalism against external threats seeks to resolve is deeply rooted in the longstanding feelings of oppression and humiliation experienced by former colonial nations. These emotions are intrinsically tied to a historical perception of the West as the 'other,' fueling a profound and enduring sense of national struggle. In former colonial nation-states, this identity crisis becomes apparent when these countries attempt to integrate into the global economy for economic advancement but soon realize that they are relegated to roles as mere suppliers of raw materials and providers of cheap labor to Western powers. Faced with the constraints imposed by neoliberal policies, the elites in these states might resort to nationalist rhetoric to assert a stronger national identity or enhance their position in the global economic hierarchy, despite their disadvantaged economic status. For example, in Zambia, the implementation of neoliberal policies, particularly privatization, has been marked by instances of corruption, a lack of regulatory oversight, and a disregard for the welfare of the people and the country's future. The international financial institutions thus refrained from commenting on these issues. As a result, an authoritarian form of nationalism is gaining ground in Zambia, driven by pervasive resentment against these neoliberal policies (Lamer, 2005, s. 41–42).

It is erroneous to assume that humiliation is a direct consequence of economic inadequacy. A national identity crisis may occur in countries such as Japan that have experienced military defeat, particularly if the nation is expected to accept responsibility for the conflict, regardless of the country's economic advancement and global influence within the capitalist order (Sung, 2005, s. 614; Nishiyama, 2023, s. 104–106; Nakahara, 2021, s. 3–4). Nationalism tends to build the nation from the past to the future. The distinctiveness and prestige of a nation's past serve as an indicator of its prospects. Cultural chauvinism has been a significant and pervasive phenomenon throughout history, but prior to the modern era, it was largely confined to the domain of elites. As nationalism spreads through wars, it also spreads cultural chauvinism throughout society (Dunn, 1999, s. 35–36; Hervik, 2011, s. 31). Despite its successful integration into the global capitalist system, Japan continues to bear the legacy of its past actions during World War II, including allegations of war crimes. The impetus behind the resurgence of nationalism in Japan can be attributed to a collective sense of humiliation and oppression. To reclaim their narrative and assert their identity, the new nationalism in Japan has sought to rewrite and reinterpret historical events. This new historiography aims to reconstruct Japan's past through a lens of pride rather than guilt, thereby paving the way for the rise of a new form of nationalism (Kersten, 1999; Penney & Wakefield, 2009, s. 548–549; Killmeier & Chiba, 2010, s. 337).

The sentiment of insecurity, a significant aspect of the new nationalism, is accompanied by resentment in the context of defensive new nationalism against external threats. Resentment represents the fundamental emotional state associated with the traditional form of nationalism, particularly in the context of nation-state formation (Greenfeld, 1994). This insecurity manifests not in distrust of "the other," but in self-distrust in the face of the other and a sense of inadequacy. In his study on new nationalism in China and Thailand, Callahan (2003, s. 490) posits that to understand new nationalism, it is necessary to understand the insecurities of countries. For example, there is a period of so-called "national humiliation" in the collective memory of the Chinese. During this period, it was widely believed that Western imperialists sought to destroy China. This idea has exerted a profound influence on the formation of contemporary Chinese identity. There is a prevailing perception that a strong state is necessary to prevent a similar occurrence in the future (Callahan, 2003, s. 491; Boylan, McBeath, & Wang, 2021, s. 33–34).

A comparable form of defensive nationalism, driven by feelings of insecurity and deep-seated resentment, is evident in Russia. This sense of self-inflicted inferiority became particularly pronounced following the collapse of the Soviet Union (Neumann, 2013, s. 158–179). During the early Yeltsin years, Russians harbored increasingly negative perceptions of themselves, as reflected in a 1991 survey where the belief that "we are worse than everyone else" and "we have brought only negative things into the world" surged from 7% to 57%. By 1995–1996, a widespread sense of shame about the country's current state took hold, leading many Russians to view the reign of Peter the Great as the pinnacle of their national history. However, the 2000s marked a significant shift, with a resurgence of national pride and the emergence of patriotism as a key element of Russian identity. This transformation was largely driven by the state's deliberate promotion of patriotic rhetoric as a means of redefining national self-perception and restoring a sense of pride in Russia's legacy (Laruelle, 2009, s. 154–155; Heller, 2018, s. 151).

These two forms of defensive new nationalism are not mutually exclusive and can coexist with one another. In the context of defensive new nationalism directed against external threats, groups perceived as internal collaborators of imperialist powers outside can be regarded as internal threats. These groups may include specific ethnic or religious groups, educated elites, or wealthy businessmen.

Conclusion: Toward a Comprehensive Understanding of New Nationalisms

This chapter introduces a classification of new nationalism, with a focus on the emergence of new nationalist ideologies in response to global phenomena such as globalization, neoliberal policies, multiculturalism, and immigration. This classification aims to address deficiencies in the extant literature by providing a more structured framework for analyzing the diverse manifestations of new nationalism observed across various geopolitical contexts.

It has been proposed that new nationalism differs significantly from traditional forms of nationalism. In contrast to its predecessors, new nationalism emerges in a context where nation-states confront challenges to their sovereignty and identity because of globalizing forces. Whereas traditional nationalism frequently placed emphasis on racial distinctions, new nationalism tends to prioritize cultural and ethnic factors. Moreover, evidence indicates that the social base of new nationalism is not limited to economically disadvantaged groups; it also encompasses those who perceive themselves as experiencing status loss due to global economic changes.

This chapter identifies two primary types of new nationalism: separatist and defensive. Defensive new nationalism has been further classified into two categories: defensive new nationalism against internal threats and defensive new nationalism against external threats. The phenomenon of defensive new nationalism against internal threats is commonly observed in Western countries, where concerns over immigration and the perceived erosion of national identity fuel the growth of populist movements. In contrast, defensive new nationalism against external threats is more prevalent in developing nations, where neoliberal policies and the perceived dominance of Western powers are perceived as existential threats to national sovereignty and stability.

This classification provides a new analytical tool for scholars to examine the dynamics of new nationalism in greater depth. The categories presented here offer a valuable framework for exploring the diverse expressions of nationalism in the twenty-first century and their implications for domestic and international politics. Further research is encouraged to investigate how internal and external threats interact in shaping new nationalist ideologies and to examine the impact of these ideologies on political developments at both the national and global levels.

Open Balkan Initiative in the Context of "New Regionalism": Opportunities, Challenges and Results

F. Gamze Çakmak

ABSTRACT

In the present article, the "Open Balkan" initiative, which emerged as a new attempt at regional cooperation in the Western Balkans, will be analyzed within the framework of the "New Regionalism" approach. Today, rather than being a constructive part of the world order, regionalism is either associated with the return of great power politics or tends to be equated with "regional blocs" that signify the collapse of the liberal international order. Regionalism and globalization are sometimes even debated as competing visions of understanding the world. In the present study, however, the starting point will be the assumption that the process of new regionalism has developed both as a component of neoliberal globalization and as a reaction to the problems it poses. While globalization is commonly identified with integration, new regionalism is, on the contrary, interpreted as opposition to global integration. The acceptance of this sharp distinction is an obstacle to seeing the actual reality: The wave of new regionalism can neither be understood simply as anti-globalization nor as a form of the phenomenon of global integration. The main claim of the present article is that the concept of new regionalism, which emerged in the context of the consequences of neoliberal globalization, refers to regional political efforts aimed at renegotiating certain aspects of the globalization process. The "Open Balkan" initiative in the Balkans on the periphery of Europe provides an important case to analyses both this regional integration effort and the global integration effort.

Keywords: New Regionalism, Balkans, Globalization

Introduction

The Open Balkans is an initiative established to remove all obstacles to the free movement of four elements (people, services, capital and goods) in the Western Balkans and integrate the countries of the region. The concept of regional integration first emerged in October 2019 with the cooperation initiative entitled the "Mini-Schengen" launched by the leaders of Serbia, Albania and North Macedonia in Novi Sad, Serbia. Renamed as the Open Balkan in 2021, the primary objective of the initiative is to reinforce cooperation between the countries of the region in numerous areas, particularly economic. The subject that was emphasized by the leaders at each meeting was that this regional initiative would not prevent European Union membership, which is the foremost foreign policy goal of the countries in the region but would rather expedite the membership process.

However, since its inception, the initiative has been subjected to numerous backlashes and negative criticism from within and outside the region, and its viability has become questionable. The first and foremost reason for this is undoubtedly the lack of trust between the countries of the region due to their conflicts and unresolved disputes. The occasional political crises in Bosnia and Herzegovina due to the status of Republika Srpska, the dialogue process between Serbia and Kosovo, and the unresolved problems and insufficiently developed relations between Serbia and Albania, mainly dating back to the dissolution of the Socialist Federal Republic of Yugoslavia, constitute obstacles to any regional unity initiative.

Despite all the negative criticism from the countries of the region, the United States has been one of the biggest supporters of the Open Balkan initiative from the beginning. Non-governmental organizations in Serbia, such as the Open Society and the Atlantic Council, also support the Open Balkan process (Đukanović, 2022). In fact, Alexander Soros, the chairman of the Open Society, emphasized in a speech that the Open Balkan initiative would create an important opportunity to resolve longstanding conflicts in the region (Demostat, 2022). American support for this regional initiative is evident in the Washington Agreement signed with Kosovo in 2020, which commits Kosovo to join this initiative (Muharremi, 2021). However, Kosovo persistently refuses to join the Open Balkan initiative, despite its commitment to this agreement.

As can be seen, the fact that America, the leader of global hegemony, supports the regional Open Balkan initiative shows that the concept of new regionalism does not conflict with globalization, but on the contrary, the two concepts interact with each other and complement each other, which is one of the main claims of the present study. If the Western Balkan countries can develop good relations and cooperate with each other on all regional issues, it will facilitate the region's integration into the Trans-Atlantic system and its institutions. Therefore, it would not be wrong to say that any attempt to ensure regional cooperation and integration in the Western Balkans will be supported by the major global powers, particularly the United States.

In line with these explanations, in the first part of the study, an analysis of the wave of new regionalism will be made based on the assumptions related to the conceptualization of regional initiatives. It will be examined how the wave of new regionalism relates to globalization, and how regionalism is defined and conceptualized will be discussed. Following the theoretical discussions, the Open Balkan initiative, which is evaluated as an experiment in new regionalism in the following chapters, will be analyzed in all its dimensions as a case study.

The Concept of Regionalism

The concept of region is derived from the Latin word "regio" meaning direction and the verb "regere" meaning "to govern" or "to command." Over time, the concept of region has come to be used to denote a boundary or delimited area, usually a state (Söderbaum, 2003: 6). There is much debate about what constitutes a region, how its borders can be drawn and how regional projects can be operationalized. The problem of defining regions is further complicated by different approaches to regionalization (Selleslaghs & Langenhove, 2020: 148). Regions and regionalism constitute an important aspect of international politics, whether in the form of free trade zones or institutionalized cooperation between states, or in the form of collective security organizations such as NATO. However, there are different definitions of regions and regionalism in the literature, and the same concepts are used to denote different processes and phenomena. As Söderbaum points out, "One of the key features of regionalism studies is that regionalism means different things to different people in different contexts and time periods" (Söderbaum, 2016).

In the IR literature, regionalism is sometimes used to refer to attempts to express a regional identity or to give it an institutional form (Fawcett, 2005, 27). In IR, regions are broadly understood as interconnected geographical units composed of states. Derived from this, regionalism policies refer to "common policies and understandings agreed upon by the members of these units" (Fawcett, 2017, 98). According to another general definition, regionalism is primarily "a state-led process for the creation and maintenance of formal regional institutions and organizations between at least three states" (Börzel & Risse, 2016: 7). Formal regional integration, on the other hand, "refers to processes where states go beyond the removal of barriers to interaction between their countries and create a regional space subject to certain common rules" (Best & Christiansen, 2016: 402). In this specific sense, regionalism is associated with a program and strategy leading to the construction of formal institutions (Hettne & Söderbaum, 2000, 457). Such processes can create interdependence as well as "perceptions of deepening common interests and identity, including self-awareness as a region" (Best & Christiansen, 2016, 402).

According to Fawcett, while the term regionalism is related to the above definitions, it is "often used to refer to less formal, often undirected economic and social activity in a particular region." Over time, this definition has been reframed to include more informal or formal processes, state and non-state actors (Fawcett, 2017, 98). In this framework, regional agreements encompass different mixes of economic, social, political and security interests. Increased interaction and cooperation on these common policies and understandings is sometimes the result of state-driven policies characterized by security concerns, while in other cases increased interaction can be the result of market-driven policies (Best & Christiansen, 2016, 402).

Most theorists adopting the New Regionalism approach define regionalism as ideas, identities and ideologies related to a regional project, while regionalization is often defined as the process of regional interaction that creates a regional space (Söderbaum, 2003, 7). The new literature on regionalism, in which the New Regionalism approach is increasingly prominent, no longer conceptualizes regions in terms of geographical proximity, but in terms of purposeful social, political, cultural and economic interaction between states inhabiting the same geography (Acharya, 2007, 634). The aim of regionalism is to pursue and promote common goals in specific areas. In this way, regionalism "ranges from promoting a sense of regional awareness or community (soft regionalism), to strengthening regional groups and networks, to whole- or sub-regional groupings formalized by interstate arrangements and organizations (hard regionalism)" (Fawcett, 2004, 433). Regionalism, which is conceived as a policy and political project, can therefore operate both above and below the level of the state. Today, therefore, a successful regionalist project presupposes emergent linkages between state and non-state actors. (Fawcett, 2004, 433).

Old and New Regionalism

Old regionalism and new regionalism are often distinguished by referring to different historical waves (or generations) of regionalism. Some theorists refer to the protectionist tendency of the 1930s, associated with "autarkic blocs," as the first major wave of regionalism. Others argue that the first wave of regionalism can be traced back to the nineteenth century, when great power (balance) politics and spheres of influence marked international politics. The Cold War, which is the period when cooperation tended to revolve around two rival blocs and thus had a curbing effect on regionalism (Fawcett, 2017, 98), is also the period when regionalism began to be conceptualized and articulated. European regionalism emerged from the ashes of two world wars that brought the European continent to the brink of destruction. The first generation of regional integration studies, as seen in David Mitrany's "*A Working Peace System,*" tended to see the nation-state as the problem, not the solution, to establishing a lasting peace that was not reduced to the balance of great powers. European regionalists such as Jean Monnet and Friedrich Schuman were driven by a normative desire to prevent another European conflict by taming the nation-state and its desire for absolute sovereignty (Acharya, 2018a, 95). The main mechanism to achieve this was to re-establish the "Westphalian" link between territorial sovereignty and social needs based on institutions and social functions for specific areas. The systematic examination of the integration process of the European Community, which began in the 1950s and evolved into a new political structure, paved the way for the institutionalization of regionalism studies. As Hurrell notes, the theoretical analysis of regionalism developed alongside the theories that sought to explain the establishment and development of the European Community (Hurrell, 1995b, 45).

In this period, the concept of regionalism was mostly used to refer to the phenomenon of integration that emerged because of economic and social interaction in a particular region (Haas, 1958). In other words, the concept of regionalism refers to increased cooperation and interdependence in a range of areas from regional trade to security to the extent of regional integration (Best & Christiansen, 2016, 402; Nye, 1968). In this framework, the establishment of regional institutions and regimes—rules that shape states' expectations and facilitate collective action—has been characterized and studied as an important part of regionalism in world politics (Hurrell, 1995a; Nye, 1971).

Theories such as neofunctionalism have argued that regional economic integration can lead to increased levels of peace and prosperity. In this respect, the European Union (EU) has come to represent the most equipped and advanced paradigmatic model of regionalism.

However, the definition and scope of regionalism associated with EC integration does not represent the full dynamics of regionalism during the Cold War. Therefore, the understanding of the regionalism dynamics of the Third World or the postcolonial world at that time remained well outside the interest and explanatory framework of mainstream approaches. According to Acharya (2018b), the limitations of mainstream theories of regionalism during this period are related to the different sources of motivation behind regionalization dynamics.

During the Cold War, the common characteristic of Third World regionalist movements was that they were anti-imperialist and anti-hegemonic. They were associated not only with national independence movements but also with the rejection of the collective hegemony of the great powers over the weak (Acharya, 2018b, 156). In these ways, regionalism overlaps with Third-Worldism, which emerged as a political alternative to colonialism and the hegemony of the two superpowers in the context of decolonization after 1945 (Pasha, 2013: 148). To the extent that these regional developments linked national independence (the war against imperialism) with social transformation, they also challenged dominant explanations of *"underdevelopment"* and the liberal political project associated with the modernization theory (Weber & Winanti, 2016, 393). In this sense, regionalism was seen as a means to address and solve the social, economic and political needs and challenges for all regions—especially those that would later be defined as the "Third World" (Acharya, 2018b, 158).

Acharya describes the idea that the world order should be governed by a series of regional groups, each under its own local great powers, as "hegemonic regionalism" (2018b, 158). Acharya also points out that "non-Western regionalist ideas and institutional forms are more progressive and emancipatory than European Cohesion, which is often seen as a precursor to European regionalism." Accordingly, whereas European Cohesion was essentially a conservative and counter-revolutionary form of regionalism, opposed to parliamentary democracy and revolutionary and national movements, regional ideologies in Asia, Africa and Latin America were oriented toward achieving national independence in the context of anti-colonialism, preserving sovereignty, achieving social transformation and challenging the domination of great powers (Acharya, 2018b, 156). Ironically, and contrary to the claims made by Postcolonial approaches that would rise after the 1980s, the non-Western regionalist movements that came to prominence from the early twentieth century to the 1970s, insofar as they linked struggles for national independence to social revolution, were the true heirs of the European Enlightenment (which predicted that all societies could be liberated on the basis of science and reason).

Previous theories of "old regionalism" regarded regionalism as a state-managed phenomenon. This attitude simplified the definition of the macro-region as an outcome of cooperation between a group of neighboring states (Hettne, 2003, 23). The previous approach to regionalism (old regionalism) was often conceived as an endogenous process. The dominant approach was the theory of Neofunctionalism, which essentially envisaged a diffusion from economic integration to political union. The New Regionalism approach goes beyond the dynamics of spillover effects to include security, social and cultural issues. The rise of regionalism was not necessarily conceived by regional actors. However, the political will to establish a regional coherence and identity ("a trans-local 'unity'") is seen as key in the new understanding of regionalism (Hettne, 2003, 28).

Old regionalism is often specific in terms of goals and content, focusing on preferential trade arrangements and security alliances[1]. New regionalism, on the other hand, varies considerably in number and scope. Compared to old regionalism, which was Eurocentric and narrow, new regionalism is both global and pluralistic (Söderbaum, 2003, 4). It is notable for being less state-centric and encompassing an ever-expanding range of actors and issues. Another difference is that whereas old regionalism acknowledged the dominant role of hegemonic actors (or "hegemonic regionalism" created "from

---

[1] The North American Free Trade Agreement (NAFTA), the European Free Trade Association, the European Economic Community, the Southern Common Market (MERCOSUR), and the Council for Mutual Economic Assistance (COMECON), which are built on preferential trade arrangements, and the North Atlantic Treaty Organization (NATO), the Central Treaty Organization, the Southeast Asia Treaty Organization, and the Warsaw Treaty Organization (Warsaw Pact), which are built as security alliances, are the best-known examples of old regionalism.

outside" and "from above"), new regionalism emphasizes the "autonomous" nature of regionalism created "from within" and "from below." Moreover, in new regionalism, the creation and maintenance of regional institutions does not depend on the dominance of a single power. Instead, the sources and agency of ideas and approaches to regional order are distributed and shared among actors (Acharya, 2018b, 81).

Regionalism is sometimes viewed as the antithesis of universalism (associated with globalization), but the two can be complementary. For example, organizations such as the European Union (EU) and the African Union complement the role of the United Nations (UN) in peacekeeping, humanitarian operations and conflict management (Acharya, 2017, 80). While regions and regionalism are important trends in world politics, "regional worlds," as Acharya puts it, "are essentially a metaphor for capturing the multifaceted, intersecting foundations and drivers of the global order" (Acharya, 2018a, 82).

Most scholars in the field emphasize the fundamental difference between the old bipolar Cold War context of old regionalism and the current post-Cold War context in which new regionalism has developed. While there are many different interpretations of the definition of this new context and its implications for regionalism, there is a strong consensus that new regionalism is an "outward-looking" rather than an "inward-looking" process (Söderbaum, 2003, 5).

The main reason why the New Regionalism approach is called "new" is that it does not focus on the integration phenomenon that took place in Western Europe between 1950 and 1970, but on the regionalization dynamics in world politics that started to take shape in the late 1980s. In other words, unlike the "old" regionalism that emerged in a specific historical context, such as the bipolar structure of the Cold War, the "new" regionalism emerged in a new structural context in which the Cold War-era structure of international politics ended, and world politics was transformed. In this sense, new regionalism stems from the structural transformations of the global system since the 1980s.[2]

---

[2] The most prominent of these structural transformations can be listed as follows: The shift of the bipolar Cold War structure and alliance systems toward a multipolar structure; the relative decline of US hegemony (regionalism and multipolarity are in fact two sides of the same coin); the restructuring of global political economy into three major trading blocs (NAFTA, MERCOSUR, EU, and Asia-Pacific until 2020) based

Structural changes constituted the sources of the differentiation between new regionalism and old regionalism. In this context, according to Hettne, the main differences between old and new regionalism can be summarized as follows: While old regionalism developed in the context of the bipolarity of the Cold War, new regionalism is taking shape in the context of globalization and a multipolar world order. While old regionalism was created "from above," new regionalism has been a relatively more voluntary process, originating from within the emerging regions. In new regionalism, constituent states and other actors have experienced an "urge to unite," in the sense of the imperative to cooperate to deal with new global challenges, or to consolidate sovereignty. In economic terms, old regionalism was inward-looking and protectionist, while new regionalism is often described as "open" and thus compatible with an interdependent world economy. While old regionalism was concerned with relations between a group of neighboring nation-states in the sphere of economics or security, new regionalism formed part of a global structural transformation or globalization in which various non-state actors operate at various levels of the global system (Hettne, 2003, 23–24).

Seeking to conceptualize the changes mentioned above, the literature on new regionalism criticizes the state-centrism of the "old regionalism" that emerged in Western Europe after the end of the Second World War. It emphasizes the social construction of regions, the role of markets and civil society actors, and the importance of capital and trade flows. Therefore, the New Regionalism approach does not evaluate the new forms of regionalism from a purely state-centered perspective. Nevertheless, most empirical studies analyze regionalism as the construction of interstate institutions at regional, interregional and transregional levels (Börzel, 2016).

The regional and interregional order that will emerge because of the above-mentioned processes will be, in Hettne's words, "structurally different from Westphalia and an alternative to *unilateralism*. It could be called 'regional multilateralism', a world order based on institutionalized constructive relations between moderately inward-looking and partially

---

on different forms of capitalism; the transformation of the Westphalian nation-state system and the associated transformation of the concept of sovereignty; the globalization of production, finance, trade and technology; the end of "Third-Worldism" and the articulation of developing countries into neoliberal globalization (Hettne & Söderbaum, 1998, 2).

self-sufficient global regions that can manage their own regional crises" (Hettne, 2008, 106). Moreover, many "New Regionalism theories can perhaps be considered new in that they emphasize the close relationship between regionalism and the *extra-regional environment*, especially globalization" (Söderbaum, 2003, 4). Thanks to this feature, New Regionalism constitutes a break with older theories of regionalism such as Neofunctionalism, which treat regions as isolated from the outside world and often tend to ignore the global environment.

To conceptualize the dynamics of the aforementioned new regionalism, authors adopting the New Regionalism approach have drawn on post-positivist theories and approaches that have challenged mainstream theories in IR since the 1980s. In this framework, New Regionalism is based on the arguments put forward by Constructivist approaches in particular regarding the way in which interests, ideas and identities are formed. The most important argument in this framework is that interests, ideas and identities should not be considered as given (Söderbaum, 2003, 11). In this respect, regions and regional orders cannot be accepted as given and fixed. In other words, New Regionalism states that regions are not "natural," objective, or simply material objects. According to Hettne, regions are processes; they are under construction (or fragmentation); their boundaries are fluid. In a constructionist approach, regions come to life through intersubjective meanings or discursive practices shared between actors (Hettne, 2003, 27). According to Hettne, regions generally refer to "transnational" sub-political formations that are located within the international system and have their own dynamics. In this framework, rather than a geographical area or a regional organization, regions generally refer to a political formation of countries that share a common political and economic project and, to a certain extent, a common identity and a relationship of interdependence. In short, a region can be defined as "a group of countries with a more or less clearly shared political project" (Hettne, 1999b, 1). Because of these characteristics, it is necessary to refer to "socially constructed" regions rather than "natural regions" (Hettne, 2005, 544). Regions constantly develop and change. A region should be understood as a process and social construction. A region, like a nation, is an "imagined community" (Hettne, 2003, 28). In this sense, regions are not simply physical constants with a static quality, but rather "reflect the changing practices of people" (Katzenstein, 2005, 12).

As Acharya puts it, "from a regional world perspective, regions are not fixed geographical or cultural entities but dynamic configurations of social and political identities" (Acharya, 2018b, 80). In other words, regions are defined in terms of the ideas, meanings and purposeful actions (practices) shared by political actors in relation to a particular region. According to Acharya, the concept of regionalism generally "implies a deliberate act of creating a common platform, including new intergovernmental organizations and transnational civil society networks, to address common challenges, realize common goals, and express and advance a common identity" (Acharya, 2010, 1005). In this framework, Acharya argues that a regional world implies a "broader, inclusive, open and interactive dynamic of regionalism and regional orders" (Acharya, 2018b, 80), as opposed to the narrow and outdated regionalism of the nineteenth century. In this sense, regions are neither entirely self-sufficient isolated entities, nor are they entirely extensions of global dynamics. The exploration of regional orders is "not only about how regions self-organize their economic, political and cultural spheres, but also how they relate to each other and shape the global order" (Acharya, 2014, 647).

Acharya and Hettne point out that the forms of regionalism advocated by weaker states seek to challenge or socialize the dominance of great powers through the establishment of norms (Acharya, 1992; Hettne, 2003). In this respect, regional orders are constructed in terms of the structural influence of the hegemonic power as well as the responses of regional powers to hegemony. On the other hand, since regionalism is a political project created by actors, it can also fail, just like a nation-state project. From this perspective, a decline in regionalism can trigger the dissolution of the region itself. However, this development does not necessarily mean that the region will turn into a closed bloc. Globalization has long made such a situation of exclusion from the global economy unlikely. Regional autarky no longer seems to be an option. In fact, globalization is seen here as a major external challenge that provokes a regionalist response (Hettne, 2003, 29).

To summarize, while old regionalism refers to the phenomenon of EU integration and US-backed regional cooperation, security regimes and organizations that developed within the framework of the hegemonic liberal international order led by the United States of America (USA), new regionalism refers to regional political efforts emerging in a context of the polarizing effect of the neoliberal globalization process and the loss of hegemonic influence of the liberal international order. For example, some proponents of the US-led liberal international order are skeptical of regionalism unless it is associated with the EU or NATO. In this view, regionalism initiatives outside the scope of the liberal international order are associated with the 1930s autarkic closed blocs or the re-establishment of great power politics (geopolitical influence and habitats). However, new regionalism (at least as conceptualized within the framework of the New Regionalism Approach) is not an attempt to highlight global and social inequalities, but rather a way to reduce them (see Amin, 1998). It is not only protectionist impulses that drive new regionalism initiatives. Rather, countries may seek to form regional blocs to enter into a more "equal" relationship with global market forces, that is, to renegotiate their relations with global financial organizations such as the World Trade Organization and the International Monetary Fund, which undermine their capacity to protect themselves from unequal competition. In this framework, new regionalism encompasses both trade blocs, which are seen as "building blocks of globalization that enable states to engage more effectively with global market forces" (Heywood, 2019, 680), and "defensive structures designed to protect economic or social interests against broader competitive pressures" (Heywood, 2019, 680).

One of the basic assumptions of the New Regionalism approach is that new regionalism is an integral, albeit contradictory, part of globalization (Falk, 2003, 64). This raises the issue of how globalization should be theoretically understood. Hettne draws on Karl Polanyi's theory of economic history to understand the emergence of new regionalism in the context of the current world order dominated by economic globalization (Polanyi, 2007). According to Polanyi's approach, the expansion and deepening of the market makes the economic sphere no longer subject to social interests and negotiations, thus creating a *disembedded* economic sphere that is autonomous from social responsibilities and intervention. Polanyi's main argument is that societies in which land, capital and labor are commodified, i.e., societies in which the market principle is fully dominant, are a new phenomenon that defines capitalism. The mechanisms of economic integration found in traditional markets, such as reciprocity and redistribution/division, have either weakened or disappeared with the growth of market exchange (Hettne, 2009, 32). However, since the detachment of the economy from society has socially destructive consequences, it triggers an attempt at political intervention aimed at "preserving society" or reinserting the economy back into social relations (Hettne, 2009, 32). In other words, the penetration of the market principle into all spheres of human activity and its erosion of social structures leads to the need to reinvent redistribution to provide people with the necessary social protection (Hettne, 2009, 32). The expansion of market exchange constitutes the former and social reaction constitutes the latter movement. Together they constitute a "double movement," which "includes attempts to remove obstacles to the functioning of the market economy on the one hand, and to resist its consequences for people, nature and industrial activity on the other" (Buğra, 2009, 238–239). On the other hand, as Sandra Halperin points out, the dichotomy of market versus society is problematic because "society" does not act against the destructive consequences of the market "as a whole" as Polanyi assumes. Polanyi largely ignores the class interests and politics that give rise to the detachment of the economy from society. In fact, the social reaction in question is not a protective countermovement against market expansion on the part of "'society as a whole', but a 'double movement' of ruling classes pursuing global expansion in order to monopolize opportunities for economic gain and prevent the rise of new classes [the process of democratization]" (Halperin, 2018, 911). This dynamic is particularly important for understanding the fundamental paradox of neoliberal globalization and the political responses that emerge from it, notably the new regionalization process.

Although neoliberalism advocated the withdrawal of the state from the economic sphere as a remedy to the crisis of overaccumulation, as summarized in the slogan "less state, more private enterprise," it required the use of state power in favor of capital in order to implement its free market principles (i.e., to isolate the economic sphere from social influence, as Polanyi argued) (Kiely, 2018). Neoliberalism is therefore not only an economic doctrine reducible to market fundamentalism; it is also a political doctrine that shapes the structures and processes of society in favor of capital (Lane, 2015, 4). Therefore, while it is true that neoliberal globalization has transformed state sovereignty to ensure the free flow of capital, this should not necessarily be understood as eroding or reducing the power of the state. Rather, there is a transformation in the role of the state. As Hettne puts it, "by implementing the ideology of globalization, the state has in effect become the disciplining mouthpiece of external economic forces rather than the protector of its own society" (Hettne, 2010, 43). In this framework, neoliberalism is understood less as an economic doctrine than as a political strategy of accumulation developed to protect capitalism from the interference of democratic politics (Slobodian, 2023). On the other hand, the globalization promoted by neoliberalism usually highlights only the processes of time-space compression, increased interdependence and global integration as the main features of globalization, obscuring the underlying political and economic content of these processes. In fact, "globalization is driven by political and economic interests based on a neoliberal perspective … supporting a particular kind of capitalism … whose dynamics are rooted in the hegemonic states of the West" (Lane, 2015, 4). Conceived in this way, neoliberal globalization has important implications for regionalism.

As a result of the practices imposed by neoliberal restructuring, production tends to shift to some specific regions of the world where it is possible to benefit from lower labor costs and/or lower primary resource costs. This phenomenon leads to the paradox of regionalization within globalization, characterized by the establishment of economically integrated regions (Talani, 2016, 211). In a context where the nation-state is incapable of managing market forces as global markets become more important, regionalism offers an effective common denominator for political governance to deal with market forces (Balaam & Dillman, 2015, 401). In this respect, regionalism can be seen as "one of the few tools available to states to try to manage the effects of globalization. If individual states no longer have the capacity to regulate in the face of uncontrolled capital flows, regionalism can be seen as a way to regain some control over global market forces and counter the more negative social consequences of globalization" (Best & Christiansen, 2016, 404).

In this sense, new regionalism refers to interventions in favor of development, security, peace and ecological sustainability, which are considered as core values (Söderbaum, 2003, 13). Hettne identifies the *pursuit of stateness*, which refers to the capacity of the state to fulfill its core functions (security and ensuring the welfare of its citizens), as an important feature of the new regionalism (Hettne, 1993, 221). Regionalism can therefore be considered both as a part of globalization and as a political response that aims to contain or manage the disruptive social effects of globalization. In this framework, regionalization represents the process of a region's transformation from a passive "subject" to an active "actor" able to express its own interests.

Attempts at Regional Cooperation in the Western Balkans

It can be said that unlike in Europe in general, the new regionalism initiatives came to the Balkans with some delay due to the conflicts that followed the dissolution of Yugoslavia and the slow economic and social transition of the countries in the region. However, it should be noted that the first forms of regional cooperation involving the former Yugoslavia emerged during the Cold War. For instance, from the mid-70s, some of the local governments in Slovenia and Croatia were involved in the Alpine-Adriatic Working Community. At the end of the 80s, the Conference on Stability, Security and Cooperation of the Countries of South-Eastern Europe (now called the Process of Cooperation in South-Eastern Europe, which has been ongoing since 1988) started an initiative like the cooperation processes in Central Europe (Đukanović, 2020, 143–147). However, despite all these initiatives, the disintegration of the Yugoslav state could not be prevented. All attempts to transform the Socialist Federal Republic of Yugoslavia into a loose and asymmetrical federation, confederation and union of sovereign states failed (RIA Documents, 1990, 11–22). On the contrary, all relations between the states were interrupted for several years due to armed conflicts. "Thus, the desire to declare and establish a national state in the post-Yugoslav region implied a clear 'demarcation' with others and reducing mutual relations and certain forms of cooperation to the smallest possible extent. Therefore, the goal of the new elites was related to the formation of new states on their own territory, without the desire to significantly link them together." (Đukanović & Dasić, 2021, 618).

However, this approach did not last long. Developments in the region and in the rest of the world after the break-up of Yugoslavia led the newly independent states to seek closer ties and cooperation with each other and with larger regional and global organizations such as the European Union and NATO. Today, the primary foreign policy goal of all the independent states that emerged after the dissolution of Yugoslavia is to become members of the European Union and NATO (except Serbia).

Until 1999, there were some initiatives for regional cooperation in the Balkan Peninsula, such as the Royamont Process and SECI. However, these initiatives, which were mainly driven by external incentives, did not have a significant impact and limited cooperation was achieved (Lakićević, 1999, 401–413).

By 1999, the international community, notably the United States and the European Union, initiated the formation of the Stability Pact for Southeast Europe in Sarajevo (Lopandić & Kronja 2010, 76–77). The aim was to first consolidate the post-conflict situation in the war-ravaged region and then to emphasize the European agenda and Euro-Atlantic perspectives of the states in this part of Europe (Busek & Kühne, 2010, 473–628). The original internal framework of the Stability Pact for Southeast Europe envisaged the existence of three working tables, thematically covering democracy and human rights, economy, development, cooperation and security. During the same period there were many failed regional cooperation initiatives. However, by 2006, experts from Europe and the region presented a report in which they drew attention to the inadequacy of regional cooperation and suggested that the Stability Pact for Southeast Europe should be revised (SRGSPSEE, 2006, 7). The recommendations presented in this document necessitated the establishment of the Regional Cooperation Council (RCC), which was envisaged to bring other regional initiatives under the same umbrella. It was emphasized in the document that the establishment of this council would be modeled on the Council of the Baltic Sea States. The members of the Council already include member states of the European Union and NATO. As can be understood from the whole process, the purpose of the establishment of the RCC is to facilitate the integration of the member states into the Euro-Atlantic system by strengthening cooperation among them in areas such as infrastructure, economy, security, human resources, justice and internal affairs.

However, the European Union insisted on the need to establish a free trade area to complete the Euro-Atlantic integration of the region and envisaged the establishment of the Western Balkans Free Trade Area based on the CEFTA agreement adopted in 1992. However, due to Croatia's objection to the Western Balkans nomenclature, the CEFTA model and name was copied with some additions in 2006 to differentiate it from the original arrangement for Central European countries (Legović, 2006). The experiences of the former Eastern Bloc countries, initially Poland, the Czech Republic, Slovakia and Hungary, were explicitly adopted to create a regional free trade area (Đukanović & Antevski 2008, 43–61). In 2021, Kosovo's Prime Minister Albin Kurti proposed a new arrangement to establish special relations with the European Free Trade Area, SEEFTA—South East European Economic

Area (Danas, 2021). This is because Kosovo was represented through the UNMIK administration in the agreement signed in December 2006 during the "re-establishment" of CEFTA (Đukanović & Dasić, 2021, 623).

It was not until Croatia left the Western Balkans as a member of the European Union in 2013 that the attempts at regional cooperation deepened significantly. However, after Croatia, new conditions for cooperation were created for the remaining Western Balkan countries. The focus of regional cooperation shifted from Southeast Europe to the Western Balkans (Đukanović, 2020, 151). It was emphasized that new initiatives should be established by addressing the failures and shortcomings of previous initiatives.

As a result of this approach, the Berlin Process, the most significant regional initiative launched in the Western Balkans prior to the Open Balkan initiative, was launched. Founded in 2014 by several European Union member states under the leadership of Germany, the Berlin Process aims to promote regional cooperation and encourage the European Union membership perspective of the Western Balkans (Serbia, Albania, Bosnia and Herzegovina, Montenegro, North Macedonia, Kosovo). The process is conducted through annual summits and numerous meetings as a platform for high-level cooperation between the leaders of the EU member states and the leaders of the Western Balkans. In addition to high-level politicians, EU institutions (European Commission, European External Action Service), international financial institutions, representatives of non-governmental organizations and the private sector in the region are also involved in the process to align the whole region more closely with the EU.

"The first founding Western Balkans Summit" of the Berlin Process, in which countries such as Austria, Bulgaria, Croatia, Greece, France, Germany, Italy, Poland, Slovenia, Slovenia and the United Kingdom participated, was held in Berlin on August 28, 2014; the second in Vienna on August 27, 2015; the third in Paris on July 4, 2016; the fourth in Trieste on July 12, 2017; the fifth in London on July 9–10, 2018; the sixth in Poznan on July 3–4, 2019; the seventh online (Sofia/Skopje) on November 9–10, 2020; the eighth on July 5, 2021, also in Berlin; and the ninth summit of the Berlin Process on November 3, 2022, also in Berlin, but this time under the new German Chancellor. The last leaders' summit of the Berlin Process took place in Tirana on October 16, 2023. The main achievements of the Berlin Process were the establishment of the Regional Youth Cooperation Office, the signing of the Agreement on the Development of the Common Regional Market and the Agreement on Regional Movement, and the creation of "green lanes" to speed up border procedures for essential goods during the COVID-19 pandemic (Trosić & Arnaudov, 2023, 60).

In the Western Balkans, located on the periphery of Europe, apart from "Open Balkan," as discussed in detail above, no regional cooperation organization based on the decisive role of local actors without the control and supervision of external actors has been established so far. Therefore, the Open Balkan is the first initiative established by the representatives of the countries in the Western Balkans.

Just before the start of the Covid pandemic, on October 10, 2019, the President of Serbia and the Prime Ministers of Albania and North Macedonia signed a declaration of intent in Novi Sad to create a "Mini-Schengen" between the three countries. (Radio Slobodna Evropa, 2019). This initiative, renamed Open Balkan in 2021, was established with the ambition to establish the four principles of freedom, namely freedom of movement of goods, people, services and capital, modeled on the European Union and the European single market. From its inception to the present day, the Open Balkan initiative has stated at every opportunity that the European Union membership obligations of the countries of the region will be respected. It has also been emphasized at every opportunity that the Open Balkan will be pursued in harmony with the ongoing mechanisms such as the Berlin Process, the common regional market, and the CEFTA 2006 agreement. It was therefore expected that Open Balkan, like other regional initiatives, would facilitate the integration of the countries of the region into the European Union and the Trans-Atlantic system.

Open Balkan: Deep Cooperation or Unsolved Problems?

In the Balkans region, which has often been characterized by political crises and instability throughout history, it is undoubtedly exciting that for the first time regional leaders are trying to establish a cooperation ground by using their own initiatives. However, since its establishment, Open Balkan has been on the agenda not only with the opportunities it has created but also with the controversies it has caused. Past and present disagreements among the countries in the region have been hindering the deepening of cooperation.

The Declaration of Intent signed in Novi Sad (Joint Declaration) advocated the elimination of border controls and other barriers to facilitate movement in the region by 2021, and sought to enable citizens of participating countries to travel within the region with only an identity card. It also envisages an open labor market for citizens of the participating countries with professional qualifications and foresees opportunities for cooperation between the participating countries, such as mutual recognition of diplomas, better cooperation in the fight against organized crime and mutual assistance in case of natural disasters.

Within the framework of the Open Balkan, several meetings and forums were organized in 2019, 2020, 2021 and 2022 (in Novi Sad, Tirana, Ohrid, Skopje, Belgrade and Niš), during which several declarations and agreements were signed.

Following is the list of the signed agreements within the Open Balkans initiative:

- "July 2021: Memorandum of Understanding on Trade Facilitation, Memorandum of Understanding on Cooperation Related to Free Access to the Labor Market in the Western Balkans, Memorandum of Understanding bon Cooperation in Protection Against Disasters in the Western Balkans.
- December 2021: Agreement on Conditions for Free Access to the Labor Market in the Western Balkans, Agreement on the Interconnection of Electronic Identification Schemes for Citizens of the Western Balkans, Agreement on Cooperation in the Areas of Veterinary, Food and Feed Security and Phytosanitary Areas in the Western Balkans, Agreement on Mutual Recognition of Certificates of Authorized Economic Operators (AEOS) Between Albania and North Macedonia, Agreement on Mutual Recognition of Certificates of Authorized Economic Operators (AEOS) Between Albania and Serbia, Trilateral Agreement on Cooperation Between General Directorate of Accreditation of the Republic of Albania (DPA), Institute of Accreditation of the Republic of North Macedonia and Accreditation Body of the Republic of Serbia.
- June 2022: Agreement on Mutual Recognition of Academic Qualifications, MoU on Cooperation in the Field of Tourism in the Western Balkans,

MoU on Cooperation in the Field of Culture, MoU on Cooperation in the Field of Tax Administrations in the Western Balkans.
· September 2022: Agreement on Food Security between the Republic of Serbia, the Republic of Albania and the Republic of North Macedonia, Memorandum of Understanding in the Field of Cinematography and Audio-Visual Activities in the Western Balkans, Agreement on Energy and Mining Cooperation, The Inter-Operational Plan on Civil Emergencies between the Republic of Serbia, the Republic of North Macedonia and the Republic of Albania." (Trosić &Arnaudov, 2023, 75–76).

Looking at the agreements signed so far under the Open Balkan initiative, it can be concluded that this is first and foremost an economic project that provides numerous job opportunities for citizens and businesses of Serbia, North Macedonia and Albania. By increasing the visibility of professional qualifications on the regional labor market, the initiative contributes to increasing competitiveness on the labor market and thus opening new job opportunities. It is also expected that the regional labor market will contribute to reducing the brain drain, which has been an increasing trend in the Western Balkans over the last two decades.

It can be argued that the Open Balkan offer opportunities for a better standard of living, economic stability and sustainability, and reduced regional security risks for the region. Nevertheless, the ongoing political conflicts in the region remain the biggest challenges to the Open Balkan and regional cooperation.

The first of these challenges is undoubtedly the fact that the foreign policy objectives of the Western Balkan countries do not coincide with each other. "Unlike the openly defined Euro-Atlantic goals and priorities of most of the Western Balkans's countries, Serbia, but also Bosnia and Herzegovina (due to the Republic of Srpska entity), are not entirely clear about their essential geopolitical commitment. The conflicts that began with Russia's attack on Ukraine at the end of February 2022 were reflected in the situation in the Western Balkans region through full harmonization regarding the condemnation of this act and the introduction of sanctions against Russia, except for Serbia, and the opposition of the Republic of Srpska entity in Bosnia and Herzegovina. As a result, the Western Balkans' already-existing mutual mistrust and antagonism have become even more extreme. Given that acute processes such as electoral reform in Bosnia and Herzegovina (failed attempts in January and March 2022) and the completely frozen dialogue between Serbia and Kosovo since 2017 have not ended, it is also questionable how much the European Union and the United States will continue to focus on the Western Balkans." (Đukanović, 2022, 2)

In addition to this division regarding foreign policy, another challenge for regional cooperation and Open Balkan is the criticism that it is *via facti* an attempt to establish a Serbian-Albanian agreement on the division of their respective spheres of interest in the Balkan Peninsula and/or the manifestation of the "Serbian World" policy or pan-Albanian efforts.(Ilić, 2021) The parallelism of regional cooperation policies in the European environment, such as the Open Balkan, on the one hand, as well as the emphasis on these types of pan-national policies, create resistance among many actors in the region. (Jovićević, 2022) The most evident instance in this regard is the resistance to the Open Balkan in Montenegro and, to some extent, in Bosnia and Herzegovina from the Bosniak and, to a lesser extent, the Croatian public. This type of dichotomy, as well as frequently contradicting messages associated with the European Union's vision of regional cooperation, produce public confusion and more radical internal forms of resistance. Therefore, the issue of (non) accession to the Open Balkan is considered a key national problem that affects relations with other Balkan entities (Vlahović, 2021).

For example, although Albania is part of this initiative and the current Albanian government supports this process, opposition politicians such as Sali Berisha point out that the Open Balkans is not a project in Albania's interest. (Radio Slobodna Evropa, 2022) At the end of December 2021, the President of North Macedonia, Stevo Pendarovski, also expressed some reservations about the Open Balkan initiative, stating that it cannot be successful if it does not include all the Western Balkan countries. (Radio Slobodna Evropa, 2022) On the other hand, the leader of Republika Srpska, Milorad Dodik (Politika, 2022) believes that Bosnia and Herzegovina should take part in this process. At the same time, Bisera Turković, Deputy Chairman of the Council of Ministers and Minister of Foreign Affairs of Bosnia and Herzegovina, stated that he "believes in the Berlin Process and does not understand why this is needed." Regarding the Open Balkan, the Bosnian leadership is distant from the idea, while the official Banjaluka and Serb leadership seem to be in favor of Bosnia and Herzegovina joining the Open Balkan framework. However, given the divided political structure of Bosnia and Herzegovina, a favorable decision on this issue is almost impossible without the support of Bosnian and Croat colleagues.

Another challenge is the narrative, led by the political elites in Pristina, that the Open Balkan is a mechanism that contributes to the realization of the so-called idea of a Serbian world (Anadolu Agency, 2022). This criticism is questionable from the outset, as it can be established from the agreements signed so far that this is primarily an economic initiative. Another criticism raised by the Pristina authorities as a reason for not wanting to participate in the Open Balkans initiative is the alleged non-recognition of Kosovo's unilateral declaration of independence (Ekonomijaonline, 2022). However, given the fact that Pristina is already part of numerous regional initiatives together with Belgrade and that the Serbian authorities do not object to Pristina's participation in existing regional initiatives (despite the dispute over non-recognition of independence), this claim by the Pristina authorities is questionable.

As for Montenegro, the political elite in Podgorica has long distanced itself from the proposal to join the Open Balkan, claiming that Montenegro has a good chance of becoming a full member of the EU before other actors in the region, because they believed that accession to the Open Balkan would slow down the expected European integration. However, it is evident that this approach is also controversial (Vijesti, 2022). This is because even if the Western Balkan countries fulfill all the conditions for accession to the EU, there is no consensus or mechanism for the Union to absorb new member states. This is due to decades of intra-European institutional turmoil due to the existing security risks on the European continent, but also to the attitudes of the citizens of the EU member states who openly oppose the admission of new member states. Given the attitudes of EU citizens toward the enlargement policy, it is reasonable to conclude that for European politicians the admission of new member states is a highly unpopular political move at the national level. Moreover, the problems faced by the Western Balkans in the regional framework are the biggest obstacle to EU membership due to the existing territorial disputes and the large number of unresolved issues that Brussels explicitly insists on resolving before the admission of new members.

Apart from the internal challenges arising from the countries of the region, the biggest external challenge facing the Open Balkan has been the war between Ukraine and Russia, which has many regional and global implications.

The conflicts arising from Russia's attack on Ukraine at the end of February 2022 were reflected in the situation in the Western Balkans region through full harmonization regarding the condemnation of this act and the introduction of sanctions against Russia, except for Serbia, and the opposition of the Republic of Srpska entity within Bosnia and Herzegovina. Consequently, the Western Balkans' pre-existing mutual mistrust and antagonism have further intensified.

As the Ukrainian crisis escalated, Serbia promptly announced the suspension of flour, oil, and other food exports at the end of February 2022, which created new problems related to the Open Balkan, but later these statements were relativized toward certain neighboring countries. Undoubtedly, the war in Ukraine also had a significant impact on the world economy and, above all, the supply of wheat. Albania and North Macedonia, as "enemy states" of the Russian Federation, together with Montenegro, are therefore in a different position compared to Serbia, which does not hold the enemy status." (Đukanović, 2022, 7). Simultaneously, there are beliefs that the Russian Federation will not be able to take advantage of this "gap" and differences between the Open Balkan members to export its products via Serbia (Komarčević, 2022). "Despite the complex geopolitical circumstances and the obvious lack of confidence in the Western Balkans, a certain optimism exists in business circles, particularly among national chambers of commerce, that the Open Balkan initiative will develop further" (Komarčević, 2022).

As a result, the perception of the Open Balkan's scope and future success cannot be perceived beyond wider regional, European, and global events and participants. It is important to remember the Russian Federation's significant influence on the political situation in Serbia and the Republic of Srpska entity. At the same time, these refer to a significant part of Montenegrin society that relies on official Moscow. "It should be emphasized that the existing concept of Russian foreign policy entails, above all, the establishment of certain reservations by South-East European countries toward NATO and also the EU" (Đukanović, 2022, 3). Therefore, any regional initiative in the Western Balkans under EU and US influence will not be supported by Russia.

Conclusion

The way regions are defined determines the membership of any regional body, the objectives of such organizations and their capacity to implement policy. In this respect, being a member of a regional body is potentially important, especially when it comes to national security and prosperity (Beeson & Murray, 2020: 3). Among the approaches that make regionalism and regionalization the focus of analysis in International Relations, the New Regionalism approach stands out. Two propositions distinguish the New Regionalism approach from the mainstream approaches that focus on regional integration in the case of the EU.

New Regionalism proposes that regional orders should be understood not as closed trading blocs or spheres of influence of great powers, but as political projects undertaken by a group of countries for the construction of a more equal and well-functioning multilateral world order. On the other hand, since multilateralism is a very ambitious form of international cooperation, it requires a strong sense of collective identity as well as shared common interests. To be successful, regions need not only to have an economic base, but also to build forms of cultural identity and political and social connections. Some key dimensions of regionalism are cultural identity, degree of economic and political uniformity and security order. In this context, the ability to resolve regional conflicts/disputes without extra-regional intervention is particularly important.

In this context, it is obvious that the Open Balkan initiative has not been very successful. Although the initiator states insist on economic integration as a priority, the discussions from the beginning of the process show the necessity of building political, social and cultural links. In the case of the Open Balkan, the most important problem and the root of the political debates is the construction of a common identity.

The regional "Western Balkan" identity has been gradually promoted since the mid-2000s but has not taken root in local societies. Moreover, this designation was seen only as a necessity in the context of the European integration of the countries of the region, without any ethnic or historical purpose. Therefore, the role models for new forms of regional cooperation were the already-existing organizations in Europe, such as the Benelux, the Visegrad Group and the Nordic cooperation. Indeed, the mandates of the Benelux countries with their forms of regional cooperation in the Western

Balkans and the Regional Cooperation Council in South-Eastern Europe are almost identical, but there are some differences regarding institutional frameworks.

Nevertheless, the biggest obstacle to the construction of a regional "Western Balkan" identity is the idea of "nationalism," which is also the most important reason for political conflicts among the countries of the region. The idea of nationalism remains the main deficiency in promoting and building a regional "Western Balkan" identity, and the handbrake for strengthening cooperation (Đukanović, 2022, 10–12). Despite the need to establish a regional union for the development of the region, some of the societies in the region do not see themselves as belonging to the Western Balkan countries, but to another identity in Europe. For example, Kosovo sees itself as a South-Eastern European country, while Montenegro and Albania adopt an Adriatic-Mediterranean identity. (Cvetković, 2021). Ironically, however, both the European Union and the United States see and assess the region as an entity, which has not yet been incorporated into the EU.

The second proposition of the New Regionalism approach is the relationship between new regionalism and globalization. The basic idea here is that regionalization and globalization form part of the global transformation and the real issue is to understand how a viable world order can emerge. The destructive social consequences of neoliberalism can create a movement of political forces aiming to halt or renegotiate the globalization process in order to guarantee territorial control, cultural diversity and human security. In this sense, regionalism, seen as the "return of the political," is closely related to governance and especially to global forms of governance. In this framework, one of the reasons for the continued relevance of regionalism is that it has the potential to promote peace, stability and prosperity as well as to solve problems of collective action.

The confirmation of this proposition can be seen in all regional cooperation initiatives, especially the Open Balkan initiative. As mentioned in the previous chapters, the biggest supporters of the Open Balkan have been the representatives of the global hegemony, namely the EU, the USA and the Open Society Foundation. This is because the difficulties brought about by the global economic crisis justified the formation of the Common Regional Market under the Berlin Process and necessitated the establishment of a regional union, now called "Open Balkans," which would create conditions for the easier movement of labor and capital. The economic and political cooperation and coordination of the Western Balkan countries in times of emergency is crucial for the healthy functioning of the neoliberal economic order. Therefore, contrary to the rhetoric of some political elites in the region (especially in Montenegro), regional cooperation initiatives such as the Open Balkan do not slow down the integration of the countries of the region into the EU and Trans-Atlantic institutions, but rather accelerate this process. Even though it is an initiative of the regional leaders, the most important goal of the Open Balkan is the full integration of the Western Balkans into the global/neoliberal economic system. Otherwise, such an initiative would not have been supported by the EU and the US.

Consequently, the Open Balkan initiative, without political coordination among the countries, based on the principle of four freedoms of movement and emphasizing only the economic dimension, is bound to fail. The Open Balkan, which is an attempt at regional cooperation between countries with different political positions and foreign policy approaches at the international level, especially emphasizing economic integration, cannot be said to have been successful so far in this context. The reason for the lack of consensus among Open Balkan members on certain political issues should be sought in the political tradition in the Western Balkans, where intergovernmental and inter-parliamentary cooperation has not taken place at the same pace. If they succeed in developing political coordination through the formulation and defense of a common foreign policy as well as economic integration within the framework of the Open Balkan, the countries of the region will become much more visible actors on the road to European integration and in world politics. This would make the process of economic integration more feasible and viable, while their positioning as a single voice in the international arena would make their foreign policy objectives more achievable and realistic. In addition, the establishment of strong cooperation among the countries of the region will contribute to the solution of the current and potential security problems in the region, as well.

Prospects for a New Form of E-Democracy: Application of Blockchain to E-Voting and New Types of Ballot Design

Arda Can Kumbaracıbaşı

Introduction

Electoral processes lie at the heart of modern representative democracies, providing the most crucial link between the people and the state, the governed and the government. These processes are inherently complex and encompass a variety of dimensions. Due to this complexity, scholars have long deliberated on what might constitute the ideal electoral system. Noticeably, on the other hand, just there are no standards for any democratic system, it is also impossible to establish universal standards for electoral rules. Electoral practices vary widely between countries, including differences in participation rules, age restrictions, eligibility for non-citizens, candidacy criteria, vote-to-seat conversion formulas, the number of seats to be filled, the structure of parliaments (bicameral vs. unicameral), methods of election, and voting procedures.

Some of the most debated topics related to elections include issues such as low voter turnout or public interest, lack of participation, lack of public awareness (which arises when people do not follow politics closely or lack a basic understanding of party positions on key issues), questions of election fairness, lack of trust in the results, and concerns about the security and supervision of electoral processes. Additionally, the classic debate over fair representation versus strong and effective governance continues to persist. It is widely understood that fair representation is more likely to occur in proportional representation (PR) electoral systems, where seats are allocated in proportion to the votes received, allowing smaller parties a chance to enter parliament and even form coalition governments. However, while PR systems often result in coalition governments, this can delay or hinder governmental effectiveness in policy making. Majoritarian electoral systems, on the other hand, can produce strong and efficient single party governments but they often tend to punish smaller parties for the sake of effectiveness. This leads to legislative-executive fusion, where the government dominates the parliament by controlling a majority, thus creating a very strong but potentially unrepresentative political environment.

In presidential systems, other issues may also arise. One is "temporal rigidity," where it becomes challenging to remove an elected president, requiring the public to wait until the next election cycle if dissatisfied. Another issue is the "executive-legislative deadlock," where policymaking can stall if there is a standoff between the legislature and the executive, especially if the president is from one party while the other in opposition controls the legislature. With no supreme institution to resolve such disputes, the entire political process can suffer.

This chapter explores the potentials for new forms of e-democracy, toward which the world appears to be evolving and that can revolutionize electoral processes around the globe. Within this framework, it proposes solutions to many of the above challenges through an innovative electronic voting model that enhances public involvement in decision making drastically. These models combine elements of representative democracy with features of older, direct democratic systems. Previously, direct democracy was deemed impractical in large modern societies (perhaps apart from referendums), primarily due to population size, as it would demand significant effort, time, and resources. However, in contemporary societies, nowadays, with the advent of internet, mobile smart phones, tablets, laptops, smart TVs, smart watches and social media, it seems that involving people in the decision-making process might be much easier than it has ever been before (Campbell et al., 2014). Another factor that was recently added to those advances is the introduction of novel artificial intelligence (AI) designs that could work further toward implementing automation strategies. The public would be able to access top level governmental debates/questions and make their choices at anytime, anywhere with a click from their electronic devices. Therefore, the public could access high-level governmental debates and cast votes from anywhere, anytime, on their devices. Such an e-voting system would allow individuals to participate in numerous political issues rather than being limited to voting for parties, leaders, candidates, or representatives.

The aim of this chapter is fourfold. Firstly, it aims to discuss the history of e-voting and existing systems, focusing on their functionality and the common challenges they face, suggesting the importance of converging into e-voting systems for the sake of ease and more efficient decision making while involving the public in politics more frequently. Secondly, it will examine how e-voting and new ballot designs can address the current problems of electoral systems. The probabilities of new ballot designs could enhance democracy, either by incorporating them into existing systems or by constructing new set of rules. Thirdly, it will provide suggestions for the utilization of blockchain technologies, investigating their advantages in securing electoral processes, information, electoral results and other important data relating to voter preferences and demographics while establishing anonymity. In other words, it will discuss how blockchain can be adopted to e-voting to ensure maximum security and prevent any form of tampering. Incorporation of blockchain into elections and the government sector would not only increase the level of trust toward electoral processes both on the side of voters and parties, but it would also enhance political participation. Increased turnout, public awareness and participation can potentially benefit any representative democratic system while providing a counterbalance to the "decline of parties" or "decline of assemblies" hypotheses.

A Rapidly Changing World

As the world shifted into a new era with developments in political culture, globalization, freer movement of people, and, finally, the internet, several ideologies emerged alongside these changes. One of those is cosmopolitanism which encompasses the idea that all human beings belong to a single global community with shared moral and political obligations that transcend national, cultural, or geographical boundaries. Cosmopolitanism challenges traditional notions of sovereignty and nationalism by advocating for global justice, human rights, and ethical responsibilities that apply universally, regardless of citizenship or state affiliation. These theories often emphasize the importance of global governance structures, international law, and policies that address issues like poverty, climate change, and inequality on a worldwide scale and promote an inclusive view that values diversity, recognizing the interconnectedness and interdependence of all people. The second idea that is closely linked to cosmopolitanism is e-democracy. Both ideas were often criticized to be too utopian. Proponents of these ideas, however, believe that with the rapid technological transformations, the world will eventually evolve into accommodating them in one form or another.

E-democracy holds a significant importance in political studies because it represents a transformative shift in the way citizens interact with government processes, policies, and political structures. Its implications reach into multiple domains of democratic theory, advocating more inclusive participation by making political engagement easier and more accessible and stronger two-way communication channels for interactivity between leaders and the public (Hall, 2012; McCormack, 2016). People can engage in decision-making processes, participate in consultations, vote remotely, overcoming barriers like time, location, and physical accessibility (Lindner et al., 2016). This addresses longstanding issues of voter apathy and exclusion. This way, the nature of political participation expands beyond traditional voting and electoral processes. Social media, online petitions, forums, and virtual town halls allow citizens to participate in new ways, influencing the political agenda, debating policies, and holding politicians accountable. It can also enhance deliberation, where citizens discuss, debate, and make decisions about public policy. Technology allows citizens to engage in more informed and aware, decentralized deliberations through online platforms, creating a more deliberative political culture. New technologies enable governments to become more transparent and facilitate the free flow of information, as citizens can easily access government data, legislative actions, and decision-making processes, improving the trust and legitimacy. This reduces information asymmetry between government officials and citizens as well as tedious bureaucracy, allowing the electorate to make more informed decisions. By using online platforms, citizens can hold public officials accountable in real-time, reporting issues, tracking the progress of government promises, and participating in feedback loops that allow for greater accountability and even enables cross-border participation. E-democracy provides political scientists with new tools to study political behavior in digital spaces. Social media platforms, for example, offer rich datasets that allow researchers to analyze how people engage in politics online, how political opinions are shaped, and how political polarization manifests in digital environments. Political parties now use e-democracy tools to run digital campaigns, targeting voters through social media, data analytics, and online advertising. This shifts the way political parties organize and strategize. Political scientists examine how these tools affect campaign dynamics, political discourse, and the overall democratic process.

Though, promoting a stronger system that enhances democratic principles there have also been numerous challenges in several areas relating to the functionality of this system. A key issue in the study of e-democracy is the digital divide—the gap between those who have access to digital technologies and those who do not. This divide can exacerbate inequalities, as marginalized communities may have less access to political engagement tools, undermining the very principle of democratic participation (Laver, 2004; Coleman and Blumler, 2009). The digital divide can limit the participation of disadvantaged and marginalized groups, such as low-income individuals, rural residents, and elderly citizens (Loader and Mercea, 2012). It is known that people with certain disabilities or the elderly can have harder time in adjusting to the technological demands of these systems (Delwit, Kulahci and Pilet, 2005). The concentration of online political engagement among more privileged groups (e.g., those with higher socio-economic status, education, or technology access) also raises concerns about unequal political influence. Another problematic area relates to false information and propaganda that can cause frequent protests that might interrupt the system or heavy ideological or issue-based polarization among public. Without a doubt, e-democracy plays a key role in organizing social movements, protests, and political activism. Digital tools facilitate collective action, from small grassroots efforts to large-scale movements and pressure governments (e.g., Arab Spring, Occupy Wall Street, Black Lives Matter). At the same time, e-democracy can contribute to political polarization. The rise of echo chambers, algorithm-driven content on social media, anonymous messaging and the manipulation of digital platforms for political gain have all led to concerns about the deepening of political divisions.

Other concerns include questions regarding AI tempering, privacy issues, questions about surveillance, leakage of information, indoctrination of under-aged groups as new ethical and legal challenges emerge. Governments and political institutions must balance the right to privacy with the need for transparency and accountability. The ability of political campaigns to micro-target specific voter groups based on detailed data has raised questions about the ethical implications of such tactics.

Meanwhile, the idea of constructing a system that can involve the whole population at any moment on vital decisions expands the horizons of democratic understanding in the modern age. Whether that be e-voting, interactions with political experts, access to information, political activism, crowdsourcing, or other forms of online referenda prove that they easily can complement or, in some cases, replace traditional forms of decision making. This brings questions about the legitimacy of government institutions, the role of elected representatives, and the potential shift from representative democracy to a hybrid or even a direct and participatory form of democracy.

Background and Seminal Studies

The idea of electronic voting is not a completely new phenomenon of course. E-voting methods have been in practice in various forms since the 1960s, involving punch-card voting machines and optical scan systems in its initial stages (Hoy, 1971). These systems allowed voters to mark ballots that could then be read electronically and while not fully electronic in today's sense, they marked the beginning of computer-assisted voting, aiming to reduce human error in counting and to increase efficiency. From 1980s onwards, the systems introduced Direct Recording Electronic (DRE) machines, allowing voters to select candidates directly on a screen, where votes were recorded digitally (Herrnson et al., 2008). DRE systems, and later in the form of electronic voting machines (EVMs), such as touchscreens or push-button systems, became more widespread in the 1990s and 2000s, especially in the US and parts of Europe. They were developed at first to simplify the counting of votes and to offer the promise of faster and more accurate voting and they were directed mainly toward voting EVMs rather than paper ballots (Storer and Duncan, 2004; Celeste et al., 2006). Even though, this paved the way for even faster counting, it also raised concerns about security of the elections and the lack of a paper trail. During that time, some countries also began experimenting with internet-based voting to allow people to vote from their homes or designated stations, especially for absentee or overseas voters (Kersting, 2012). However, challenges with internet voting, including cybersecurity risks, have limited its widespread adoption.

Several countries have experimented with e-voting over the years, attempting to modernize the electoral process, improve accessibility, and reduce errors or fraud (Kersting and Baldersheim, 2004). The outcomes have been mixed, and concerns over security, transparency, and reliability have led many to reconsider or abandon electronic voting systems (Byrne, 2017). Estonia is one of the most successful and well-known examples of e-voting and the first country to pioneer nationwide internet voting for elections in 2005 using digitalized IDs to authenticate identity of voters and cryptography systems to ensure that votes cannot be altered once cast. Estonian system is considered one of the most secure and reliable systems in the world. Voter turnout in Estonia is among the highest in Europe, and the use of e-voting has been credited with increasing participation, especially among overseas citizens. Despite the system's success, there are ongoing debates about cybersecurity and the possibility of foreign interference, especially considering global cyber threats. Similarly, Switzerland has been experimenting with electronic voting for over two decades, testing different systems in various regions, with some cantons using internet voting systems in federal elections and referendums. Despite extensive testing, the Swiss government suspended online voting trials in 2019 after concerns were raised about the system's security and several vulnerabilities were identified that could potentially compromise the integrity of elections.

The Netherlands experimented with internet voting and EVMs, used both online and machine-based voting in elections. The internet voting system was intended for Dutch citizens living abroad, and EVMs were used for domestic elections. In 2006, security experts demonstrated vulnerabilities in the systems, showing that the machines could be hacked, disputing the integrity of elections. EVMs were stopped to be used in 2007 and since then, the country has returned to traditional paper ballots for domestic elections. Online voting is discontinued, despite discussions on how accessibility and security can be improved.

The US also has seen various attempts at using EVMs since the 1990s, but these have been controversial, with concerns over security, transparency, and accuracy like other cases (Herrnson et al., 2005). A few states have also explored internet voting for absentee ballots or overseas voters. In the aftermath of the contested 2000 election, the US invested heavily in electronic voting technology, but faced similar challenges relating to hacking, malfunctioning machines, and the lack of a verifiable paper trail. Since the controversies surrounding the US presidential election of 2000, scholars have become interested in the issue of trust in the electoral process, ballot security and fraud perceptions (Alvarez et al., 2008: 755). Research has investigated the impact of new voting technologies on election outcomes (Card and Moretti, 2007; Herron and Wand, 2007; Katz et al., 2011), legal challenges to electronic voting (Hasen, 2005; Judis, 2001; Tokaji, 2007), the impact of new voting technology on voter confidence (Alvarez and Hall, 2008; Alvarez et al., 2008, 2009; Atkeson and Saunders, 2007; Bullock et al., 2005; Murphy et al., 2007; Stein et al., 2008), and the fairness of the electoral system more generally (Claassen et al., 2013; Hasen, 2005; Beaulieu, 2016: 18–9). The 2020 US election saw widespread use of paper ballots and absentee voting in response to concerns about both the security of machines and the COVID-19 pandemic. Various forms of e-voting are continued to be experimented but there is no nationwide system, and election security remains a major point of worry. Paper ballots and absentee voting are still the most widely used methods.

Brazil is another major example and has been relatively successful in utilizing EVMs rather than internet voting in national elections for over two decades (Schneider et al., 2020). Voters use EVMs with touch-screen interfaces to select candidates. These machines are not connected to the internet in order to reduce the risk of hacking. Results are transmitted securely once polls close. Brazil's e-voting system too, has faced criticism from opposition parties and election experts, debating the level of transparency and security of the machines (Avgerou et al., 2009). Schneider and Senters (2018) state that, though advantageous for voter, these systems can potentially disadvantage nonviable candidates, while viable candidates were more effective in communicating necessary information for valid ballots. According to their study, the transition to electronic voting also increased voting costs, benefiting candidates with more resources for campaigning (ibid.). Employing a regression discontinuity design, the study reveals that electronic voting significantly boosted vote shares for viable candidates, underscoring how voting technology impacts election outcomes and candidate viability (ibid.). Their findings indicate the need for impartial voting systems. Argentina has also experimented with EVMs in local and provincial elections since 2011. In some areas, digital signatures and biometric verification were introduced for voter identification.

India uses EVMs for national and state elections, and the system has been largely successful in speeding up the vote-counting process and reducing human error. Devanesan and Chandrasekaran (2011), Saraph (2011), Kher (2015), and Desai and Lee (2019) highlighted the significance of EVMs in Indian elections toward enhancing the electoral process and reducing electoral fraud. Introduced to combat issues like booth capturing and bogus voting, EVMs have transformed Indian elections into more secure, efficient, and eco-friendly events. Security features, such as tamper-proof microchips and unique identification numbers, enhance voter confidence. Like Brazil, India has also faced controversies and allegations of tampering, especially in the aftermath of tightly contested elections. There have been calls for a verifiable paper trail to ensure the integrity of results.

Delwit, Kulahci and Pilet (2005) examine the legitimacy of electronic voting in Belgium and the use of EVMs, which were introduced in 1994. Despite its implementation, there was a lack of assessment regarding voters' opinions on this method. Findings reveal that a significant majority of respondents found electronic voting easy (95.11%) and had confidence in the system (88.88%) (ibid.). The study also explored the impact of age and educational capital on attitudes toward electronic voting, revealing a partial digital divide, where older and less educated individuals expressed more difficulties and mistrust toward the system. Belgium abandoned the use of electronic voting machines in 2019.

For Ireland, using electronic ballots, voters exhibited a tendency to rank only a few candidates, demonstrating low levels of party loyalty and a preference for disapproval voting using the single transferable vote system. The data indicate a division in traditional politics, challenging the assumption that STV guarantees proportional representation (Laver 2004).

As it can be seen, when one delves into the past of e-voting, a variety of different methods can be seen. None of them worked flawlessly, however, and the greatest challenges relate to cybersecurity and integrity of elections and securing of votes. That is why, a lot of countries, such as Germany have rejected e-voting due to fears about electoral transparency and verifiability (Weill, 2017; Bund, 2016). The more contemporary adaptations of electronic voting utilized voting through internet, from home, but this also created further complications and raised further questions concerning the legitimacy of results, because securing the votes were difficult and proving that the results were not tampered with or manipulated was not easy. Several scholars (Toumi et al., 2018; Ahmad et al., 2020) have been testing methods on ways to secure e-voting mechanisms. In relation to e-voting and online engagement, cyberattacks, hacking, and the manipulation of digital platforms by foreign actors have led to the questioning of the integrity and legitimacy of online political processes (Chung and Wu, 2012).

Rheingold's early work (1993), although not exclusively about e-democracy, laid a foundation for understanding online communities and the concept of "virtual communities" that could support democratic participation, debate, and shared purpose. Coleman and Blumler (2009), in their seminal study point out the transformative potential of technology in democratic practices, arguing that internet can create new avenues for public deliberation and reduce the distance between government institutions and citizens. However, they also warn of the risks, such as digital divides and the challenge of fostering meaningful engagement rather than superficial participation as discussed above. Similar studies (Hacker and Jan van Dijk, 2000; Jenkins and Thorburn, 2003; Jefferson, 2007; Coleman and Shane, 2012) discussed the ways the internet can enhance from democratic citizenship, civic responsibilities, providing opportunities for new ways of engagement, new media's role in raising awareness, democratization of information, facilitating stronger communication between citizens and governments, participatory budgeting while also raising questions about the quality and authenticity of online participation, inclusivity, privacy concerns, technical challenges, the potential for divisions, inequalities or polarization within societies, sustainability of electronic systems, and questions about the impact of online political engagement versus offline action. Putnam's (2000) arguments on how civic engagement is essential to democratic health, and the decline of traditional forms of community engagement has weakened democratic participation laid the groundwork toward how the digital age can be utilized to foster genuine engagement and community building, rather than isolated or passive forms of participation. Scholars such as Lessig (1999), Bowler and Donovan (2016), and Gerbaudo (2012) also claim that internet infrastructure and software design impact democratic processes, suggesting that technological architecture can either promote or restrict freedoms in digital spaces, spelling concerns about design, accessibility and usability. In exploring different models of online voting, digital public consultation, and crowd-sourced decision making, offering a pragmatic perspective on how to design systems that enhance democratic engagement; the authors (ibid.) emphasize the need for user-friendly interfaces and transparent processes to ensure public trust. Gerbaudo's (2012) study of the Arab Spring protests illustrates the power of social media and digital tools in mobilizing political movements on how digital platforms can facilitate political engagement in authoritarian contexts.

Blockchain and Secure Voting

Perspectives on e-voting showcase the potential to revolutionize electoral systems by offering more secure, low-risk, efficient, and inclusive voting methods if it can be protected with an impregnable method. The security provided by blockchain systems makes it a strong option for revamping the e-voting technologies to be secured by blockchain. On the other hand, Blockchain-based elections has not been adopted widely around the world yet. Recently, mobile voting and blockchain-based voting systems have been explored successfully in South Korea and parts of US, like West Virginia in 2018, used blockchain technology for military personnel voting abroad, aiming to create a secure, tamper-proof voting system. These technologies remain experimental, but they have shown potential in pilot programs. Due to concerns over security and transparency, recent systems often combine digital interfaces with a voter-verifiable paper audit trail, ensuring that voters can confirm their choices on a printed ballot before it is stored for recounts or audits (Iansiti and Lakhani, 2017).

Various studies (Wattenhofer, 2016; Sarmah 2018) investigate how blockchain systems can enhance security, reliability, availability, transparency, validity and record keeping; as well as how these systems can be strengthened. Voter anonymity and secrecy, securing remote voting, transparency of electoral results and improved election verifiability seem to be the most important elements to be consolidated for properly functional electronic elections (Krimmer et al., 2021; Alvarez and Hall, 2008; Johnson, 2004). Popoveniuc and Vora (2010) emphasize that voter-verifiability is crucial, enabling voters to confirm their ballots while increasing familiarity and privacy by using end-to-end and back-end systems. Democracy aims at decentralizing political power and blockchain at decentralizing currency, business, finance and other aspects of daily life—therefore, decentralized governance in the virtual world faces many of the same problems in the real world as well (Magnuson, 2020: 195).

> One main theme that is addressed in several articles and reports is democratic backsliding and its impact on elections. This is not surprising considering that several scholars have noticed, since the 1990s, a "democratic recession" (Diamond 2015), a "third wave of autocratization" (Lührmann and Lindberg 2019; Hellmeier et al. 2021). Mechkova, Lührmann, and Lindberg (2017) reveal that most change over the past four decades has occurred among authoritarian countries which used to be overwhelmingly closed autocracies but have become electoral autocracies. This process of backsliding electoral democracy often involves much more than blatant election-day vote fraud (Lührmann and Lindberg, 2019). Levitsky and Way (2002: 53) note that in competitive authoritarian regimes, elections are generally free of massive fraud but "incumbents routinely abuse state resources, deny the opposition adequate media coverage, harass opposition candidates and their supporters, persuade members of opposition parties to switch party, gerrymandering, centralizing party leadership, limiting new parties to attend election, and in some cases manipulate election results." Hence, one process of democratic backsliding can be described as the strategic manipulation of elections (Magnuson, 2020: 414, 424).

So, one argument would be on how public can be made more aware and participant while enhancing electoral processes, trust in governments-leaders-regimes, and securing and providing transparent electoral results using electronic means. The literature on blockchain covers some of the emerging trends in search of a more secure and transparent e-voting system, and how blockchain's decentralized nature could prevent tampering and increase transparency, making it a strong and viable alternative to traditional voting. Everything that has stayed analog, including property rights and identity, can now be created and maintained online. Blockchains are powerful tools because they create honest systems that self-correct without the need of a third party to enforce the rules. They accomplish the enforcement of rules through their consensus algorithm. They achieve unbreakable security through establishing three core principles: decentralization, cryptographic hashing, and consensus mechanisms (Zeng et al., 2022; Drescher, 2017; Gates, 2017) which is an enormous leap for security of e-voting. These decentralized systems create a distributed network of nodes where information is not stored on a single server but a large multitude of computers. Every node has a copy of the blockchain, making it extremely hard for a single party to alter the chain, removing the human factor. Any transaction or change must be verified by multiple nodes, reducing risks of data manipulation and creating a transparent, tamper-evident ledger. Moreover, each transaction is connected to the previous one, making it extremely difficult to alter a node without affecting the others in the network. Each blockchain has its own algorithms for creating agreement within its network on the entries being added. There are many different models for creating consensus because each blockchain is creating different kinds of entries. Some blockchains are trading value, others are storing data, and others are securing systems and contracts.

Theoretically, if a single entity could control over 50% of the network's computational power (known as a 51% attack), they could manipulate transactions by reversing or halting them. This attack is challenging and costly to execute on large, which makes it very hard to break. Secondly, each block in a blockchain contains a unique cryptographic hash of the previous block, creating a chain where every block depends on its predecessor. This linkage means that any alteration to a block's data will also change its hash, breaking the chain and alerting the network. This makes tampering with blockchain data difficult, as altering one block requires recalculating the hashes of all subsequent blocks. Hashing algorithms themselves are very secure, but if a theoretical quantum computer capable of massive parallel processing became available, it might be able to solve the cryptographic hash functions quickly enough to alter blocks. This remains a speculative risk and a topic of research. Finally, protocols like proof-of-work (PoW), proof-of-stake (PoS), and others ensure that transactions are validated by network participants in a secure, transparent, and fair manner, making it very difficult for a single malicious actor to manipulate the blockchain.

Several approaches to utility blockchain methods have raised some crucial points that need consideration. To reinforce the immutable nature of blockchain applications robust security measures should be implemented, such as encryption, firewalls, authentication protocols, regular security audits and tests to identify vulnerabilities/threats (Drescher, 2017). Utilizing open-source software, publishing detailed reports on the design, testing, and operation of e-voting systems, conducting independent audits and verification of election results can enhance transparency and accountability. Immediate and effective measures need to be implemented for penalties or judicial intervention if there is a problem in the voting process or counting of votes. E-voting systems should be designed to ensure all citizens, including those with disabilities,

Table 7.1. Previous Approaches to Utilizing Blockchain Methods (Bulut et al., 2019: 2)

Architecture and Design	Security Considerations	User Authentication
• Blockchain permission • Maintain data integrity	• Data integrity • Digital Signature	• Asymmetric authentication
• Smart contract • POA Permissioned blockchain • Exonum, Quorum and Geth Frameworks	• Secure authentication via identify verification • Does not allow to trace voters from votes • Transparent	• Identity verification service
• Multi-tiered • Two Factor Authentication • Encryption based on public-private keys	• User authentication • Monitoring and auditing for data integrity • Risk of voter to forget their ID, password	• Randomly generated password to use on polling station
• Zcash tokens • Authentication with Challenge-Handshake Authentication Protocol	• Anonymity • Privacy • Transparency	• Challenge-Handshake Authentication Protocol (CHAP) • The voters' email addresses
• Smart contract on Ethereum	• Anonymity	• Asymmetric authentication

limited digital literacy or people who have not access to digital technologies, can participate in the voting process. This can be achieved through the provision of accessible interfaces, user-friendly design, and support services for those who require assistance. Educating the public about the benefits and risks of e-voting is essential to increase awareness and trust in the voting process. Citizens should be provided with clear and concise information about the voting process, including how their votes will be counted and the security measures that are in place. Collaboration between stakeholders (i.e., governments, election officials, technology vendors, and civil society organizations), is essential for designing and implementing effective e-voting systems (Gates, 2017). Immaculate and secured record keeping of the votes, transactions and results is another crucial aspect of voting. These records can be secured, recorded, verified, and traced by blockchain as well. Once votes are recorded or cast on blockchain, they can no longer be deleted or modified. Therefore, blockchain's transparency can boost public trust, as votes are recorded on a publicly accessible ledger that cannot be altered without detection (Kiayias and Lazos, 2022). Researchers often emphasize the benefit of voter-verifiable systems allowing individuals to confirm that their votes were counted accurately; while creating a secure, immutable ledger of votes, theoretically preventing tampering and making each vote traceable (Shahandashti and Hao, 2016). This way, blockchain system would prevent stealing or altering of votes and stop hackers (Figure 7.1).

> To manipulate votes, hackers would need to access the system as a citizen within the proposed solution. However, a citizen can only vote once. When a citizen casts a ballot, the e-government system is notified without revealing any information about the identity of the vote. The system then marks that person as having voted. Since the system obtains electorate data from the e-government, it is not possible for a person who has been marked as voted to vote again. Even if a hacker obtains a citizen's information and gains access to the system, they would still be unable to vote more than once. The ballot box information, along with the list of candidates and the relationship between citizens and the ballot box, will be provided by the government, which is the trusted party in the elections. After a citizen casts their vote, it will be added to the blockchain, and each vote will be guaranteed by the system to be immutable. Since the blockchain contains all citizen votes anonymously, the official results can be announced within minutes after the election concludes. If the whole country would have been represented with a single blockchain, synchronization of the system would have a performance issue due to abundance number of ballots and the distance between voting centres. So, to decrease latency, chains are distributed over levels. At the lowest level, there will be a chain that consists of nodes (machines / voting centers) where citizens will perform their voting about election. Due to the relatively a smaller number of nodes in the system, synchronization will take affordable amount of time at the lowest level. (Bulut et al., 2019: 2–3).

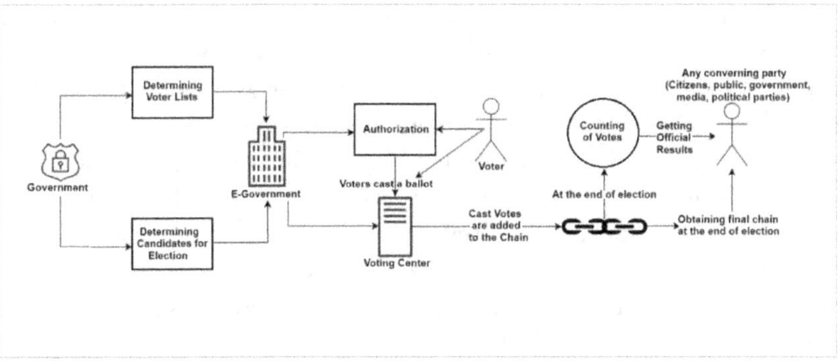

Figure 7.1. Application of Blockchain to E-Voting Process (adopted from Bulut et al., 2019: 3)

Political parties or NGOs can also use blockchain-based systems to securely and transparently record and track information such as donations, expenditures, and membership data. These systems can help to ensure that finances, budgets, expenditures, internal elections, primaries, electoral campaigns, donations are transparent and tamper-proof and can be audited and verified by anyone. Transparency in funding of party campaigns, would enable donors to track the use of their donations and ensure they are being used for their intended purposes. This could increase trust and accountability between donors and parties. Blockchain technologies can help political parties to streamline administrative processes and reduce costs by eliminating the need for intermediaries and reducing the risk of fraud and corruption. According to some studies (Hsiao et al., 2017), utilizing Elliptic Curve Cryptography, Ring Signatures, and Signcryption, efficiency and security can be enhanced while minimizing costs, allowing voters to cast their votes via mobile devices, providing accessibility and convenience.

Challenges and questions surrounding the implications of blockchain remain. De Filippi and Wright (2018) argue that blockchain can potentially shift voting systems toward greater public choice by enabling more participatory and transparent democratic processes. However, they emphasize that these advantages depend on resolving issues around privacy, confidentiality, scalability, and voter accessibility. They suggest that blockchain-based voting may be best suited for specific use cases, such as referenda or local elections, where lower turnout and scale reduce the risks associated with blockchain limitations (ibid.).

Maintaining voter anonymity while preserving transparency is a major challenge (Chang and Lee, 2006). Techniques such as homomorphic encryption, zero-knowledge proofs, and ring signatures are frequently cited as ways to encrypt votes securely without revealing voter identities, but practical implementation remains challenging (Shahandashti and Hao, 2016). Blockchain networks may face scalability issues, especially in large-scale elections (Kiayias et al., 2017). They also could inadvertently exclude people without digital access or those who are uncomfortable with complex digital systems. Literature in this area emphasizes that inclusive design, education, and access are essential if blockchain-based e-voting systems are to serve the general population equitably.

Since blockchain networks operate on self-governing principles or decentralized governance, questions arise about who maintains the network and addresses problems that might arise (Walch, 2019). This is especially pertinent for public, government-controlled elections, where voters expect accountability. Decentralized and distributed systems can be used to eliminate the risk of a single point of failure. This means that there is no central point of control, which makes it difficult for hackers or malicious actors to compromise the system. While blockchain is often touted as decentralized, it can be influenced by powerful miners, developers, and stakeholders who have significant control over the network (ibid.). Some researchers argue that government-run blockchains or private-public partnerships may be necessary for widespread e-voting. Networks, especially those based on proof-of-work (PoW) consensus mechanisms, consume significant energy. This has raised questions about the sustainability of blockchain-based e-voting, especially for large-scale national elections. Alternative consensus mechanisms like proof-of-stake (PoS) are being considered, though they come with their own trade-offs in security. A supervisory mechanism that will conduct and control the process of elections (such as the government, judiciary or an e-government software) seems to be needed, which goes against the decentralization principles of blockchains.

"Any system that attempts to decentralize power must deal with a basic problem: group decision making and its inefficiencies. Once we introduce multiple actors into the decision-making process, the possibility of disagreement and dissension arises. And if power is spread out widely, to thousands or even millions of people, these negotiations and discussions become quite difficult. You cannot simply have the entire population of the United States sit down in a forum and debate with one another. As a result, modern democracies have effectively given up on decentralizing most government decisions. Instead, citizens exert their control over government through periodic elections, delegating power by choosing representatives. Blockchain's efficiency problem is even greater: to make the technology work, a majority of all the computers on the network must reach consensus on the rules and actions taken on the blockchain" (Magnuson, 2020: 196–7). A proposed solution to this in e-voting would be to create several servers that work at electoral district level and then connect to a central one at later stages. Therefore, "we may be willing to accept the inefficiencies of decentralized decision making if other external values are more important, such as a belief in the virtues of self-government or the dignity of individual choice. John Stuart Mill, for example, argued in favor of democracy because of its effect not just on the quality of decisions but also on the moral fiber of citizens" (ibid.). Eventually, if some of those challenges can be solved, blockchain can secure elections much better than traditional physical systems.

Stages of Voting and Remedies Through New Designs

Most literature on e-voting and blockchain discusses how blockchain technologies can secure the voting process, but there is little work conducted on how current electoral systems can be reformed to address their inherent problems. Therefore, even though a transition from physical voting to e-voting may occur, the original issues persist. This section will discuss commonly used electoral systems and their perceived problems, as well as the four stages of elections, each of which presents different complications. For each electoral stage and type of electoral system, this section will explore how these problems can be alleviated using an e-voting system with a new ballot design and by developing new software options.

Considering that elections are carried out fairly and freely by adhering to the principle of universal suffrage with judicial supervision, under constitutional protection, with balanced reporting by the media, and with open and transparent counting of votes; an electoral process usually includes several elements that contribute to the results: (1) pre-electoral stage (ballot design and registration), (2) vote casting stage (ballots and polling), (3) post-electoral stage (vote securing, transporting of votes and open counting), and (4) conclusion (declaration of results and data entry, record keeping).

The First Stage

This stage involves the pre-electoral environment or the path that leads to an election. This is where party campaigns, meetings, gatherings, leader and member activities and speeches, partisan politics and candidate selection procedures take place. But most importantly, this is where voter preferences are shaped and voting behavior becomes significant. A wide range of factors can affect voting behavior. Long-term components such as economic structure of a country, historical background, social divisions, and political culture of a country can affect the level of participation, political awareness and party attachments among public. An individual's upbringing from early childhood is seen as one of the main factors that shape their future choices. Similarly, beliefs, traditions, value orientations and group loyalties that emerge during these processes can lead to the establishment of strong bonds between voters and parties that may create high levels of party identification and commitment. Short-term trends, conversely, can have more dynamic effects on voters and sway electoral results. Electoral volatility, sudden shifts in votes, last-minute decisions among indecisive voters, realignment or dealignment tendencies are often a consequence of such trends. Short-term economic conditions and change (economic voting), social and political circumstances near an election, campaign activity, influence of media, candidate images, governmental performance, protest elements (protest voting), issues in daily agenda (issue voting), and structural obstacles (such as the type of electoral system which may lead to strategic voting) can be defined as short-term trends that affect voter preferences. Apart from these major factors there can also be smaller components that may affect voting: automatic vs. manual registration; electronic vs. physical voting; the place that a voter votes (if it involves traveling or not); the day the election is held (weekend, weekday, or holiday); whether system enforces mandatory voting or not; how many times an individual has to vote (round systems can lead to voter fatigue for instance); how many candidates do they vote for; how many parties are competing in the electoral arena; do individuals believe that their vote can make a change; level of trust toward the system; and so forth.

For the state mechanism and stakeholders, this stage involves decisions on electoral rules and their application (depending on the electoral system being used), formulation of the ballot papers based on these rules, listing of candidates, preparation of ballots, securing of ballot zones by judicial supervisors, the distribution of voters according to their registration areas on where they will be voting, based on regions and population—or setting up postal voting mechanisms.

The proposed remedies for the first stage through electronic methods are numerous. By utilizing an app or a software program, long before the initiation of the elections, voters can be drawn into, participate and follow the electoral process. The app would be protected by blockchain technologies and would be connected to an e-government system where each citizen would have a unique ID number connected (like e-wallets in crypto currencies).

The app would feature two parts, one that would contain all the open information of citizens (citizens would be able to choose which information they would like to reveal) that could be used for collecting comments or demands of citizens, survey data, questionnaire answers, demographic data and statistics. The other would be kept totally anonymous for voting and other private information. This part would be encrypted and kept confidential. Such an app could feature additional and vital information on electoral rules, provide summaries on electoral rules, show geographical maps of electoral districts, contain history of election results, could feature a detailed list of each party and their programs, party manifestoes, their candidate lists (maybe also containing video messages by candidates), their intra-party electoral information, primary processes, parliamentary meetings, registration processes providing unique anonymous ID numbers for each citizen that might want to join a party as a member. At later stages, it can provide rewatchable party member or leader speeches, conventions, gatherings, election campaigns and other activities. Theoretically, apart from parties, interest groups, trade unions, NGOs can also be featured in these campaign sections of the software. So, this app could bring all the media related content under a single banner as well—where each party and actor can upload their own content for promotional purposes to connect and appeal to the voters. This would make access to information much faster. This hypothetical app could be designed to make citizens be able to join a party of their choice as members if they wish to do so or register as candidates. It could create two-way communication channels between citizens and representatives who would like to instantly bring out their grievances or demands. Advances in AI technology could be used to group up citizen demands and respond to them appropriately. This could play a major role in shaping voter perceptions, keeping them more aware, informed and participant throughout the whole process. It could also be used transparently by parties to appoint candidates and carry out their primaries in front of whoever wishes to watch while sorting out party lists. The app could also have a news section where it provides daily political news globally and locally for the public. If this software could potentially become widespread and taught to every citizen from an early age, in a short period of time it could become the major source of all political activity for citizens catering to the theories of e-democracy. Just before the elections, it can provide information on how the elections would be conducted—most likely eliminating any need for travel or physical conduct but instead making people to vote at the convenience of their homes. For the state officials, it would eliminate setting up of physical ballots, printing papers, carrying out postal services for distant voters, securing ballots, transportation of ballots and ballot papers, manual counting or physical supervision for electoral integrity. This will have obvious advantages over traditional paper-based voting systems, including increased speed and accuracy, reduced costs, and greater accessibility. Smart contracts of blockchain technologies can be used to automate the voting process, eliminating the need for intermediaries such as election officials. This reduces the risk of human error, fraud, and corruption.

The Second Stage

The second stage of elections involves the ballot structure and design. This is an important but somehow a lesser studied topic. That is mainly since each existing electoral system comes with a proposed type of ballot paper. It is often a matter of simple choice for a candidate, a party or preferential ranking of candidates and in the case of referendums a "yes-no" question. These simple designs traditionally have been thought as mechanisms to prevent voter fatigue. Meanwhile, surveys that investigate voting behavior, electoral preferences and electoral geography need detailed questionnaire designs and proper sample selections. However, surveys can be financially demanding, time consuming and require the conductors to travel great distances.

For the second stage, an e-voting system that utilizes the app mentioned above can combine the simplified approach of electoral questions (to tick the candidate/party or yes/no) while introducing an additional and optional section bearing important questions like surveys creating a middle-ground between simple elections and surveys. This will enable researchers to receive more in-depth answers from their subjects that wish to fill the additional sections, while expanding the sample size to all eligible voters who vote. Such designs will also allow protesting voters to bring up their voice by going beyond casting empty votes (and thus, separate them from absentees) but also having a section where they could write down their comments illuminating their discontent.

This method could open countless options. Instead of just choosing candidates, representatives or parties, people can be involved in decision making relating to crucial issues or points of debate. This way, the public could be involved in many referendums, binding or advisory depending on importance. This would be a strong system to create an environment of direct democracy, constant participation, interaction and support for politicians. The utilization of an app takes away most of the time-consuming aspects or financial burdens of setting up referendums. An atmosphere of negotiation, discussion and voice initiated by such a system would better uphold the principles of democracy. An AI automated system would then categorize and count the results, distribute and announce them, and securely record them.

So, no longer would people be limited to making a simple yes-no decision, but, if they wish, could go beyond, and indicate how important an issue is for them on a scale of 1 to 10 for instance—or can take a 5-question mini-survey relating to the issue. This could bring so much more insight into the mind of the people and enhance the understanding of representatives of the public's opinions. This could lower party identification based on blind loyalties and advance policy issues. It is known that more and more people are becoming aware of crucial political issues of our day due to information technologies, and they follow world events much more closely due to the advent of social media. A more interactive and participant system that is offered to the public to decide, can potentially distinguish between people who are interested in that topic that they will be voting for and those who are apathetic or uninterested.

Furthermore, this could also resolve a debate that has existed for many centuries: the concept of the "universal vote." The longstanding debate has centered around alternative proposals suggesting that people with a strong knowledge of an issue, better education, or more experience should have more voting power than those who lack understanding of the issue or the political system in which they live. Of course, this posed many questions such as: how a person's knowledgeability would be measured; who would have one vote and who would have more; how it would be decided in terms of who knows what's best and who does not. This debate can be traced back to the Ancient Greek philosophers, where their picture of an ideal society involved a system with the ones that possessed extraordinary wisdom taking the rule into their own hands. Those people were called the "philosopher kings" who would dedicate their lives to ruling the society in the best way they can. So, the idea of having some level of understanding of what one is casting their votes for and the awareness that comes along with it, is a crucial factor for a healthy decision-making environment. This is why some limitations (which may vary by country) involve age or citizenship criteria, to ensure, to some extent, a baseline level of knowledgeability. Naturally, such ideas were dismissed as elitist or as undermining the principle of equality. However, an e-voting system could potentially address this by allowing those with a genuine interest in an issue to participate, while those who are not informed can simply choose not to vote on that matter, opting instead to vote on something else that interests them. So, people with an interest on a particular issue would participate, and others that are interested in a completely different issue could choose to attend a completely different referendum. It could also allow voters to demonstrate their level of knowledge through additional questions or by asking them to score the issue based on its importance to them, and this could be factored into the vote tally. Therefore, a system based on such methods would encourage and provide constant participation on political issues by people or NGOs, whenever they wish to do so.

The Third Stage

This is the post-electoral phase, that involves the immediate aftermath of votes being cast and where electoral rules come into play. It incorporates elements such as the effects of district magnitude that decide on how many candidates will be sent into the legislature per district and mathematical formulas that decide on how votes per district are translated into seats for parties. Such formulas vary from system to system and use different methods such as Borda count, largest remainder method (that uses quotas such as Hare, Droop or Imperiali quota) or highest average method (such as D'hondt, Saint-Laguë, Imperiali, Huntington-Hill, Danish and quota methods). These structural rules can have adverse effects on election results which in turn affect the party system directly. This stage also encompasses the securing of votes physically, transporting them and counting them.

The electronic system proposed in this chapter will calculate the results and distribution of seats, save them instantly, and create secure, verifiable and traceable records. It will also provide the formulation of not only the results of votes but also the survey questions, demographic data, turnout and volatility levels as well. Blockchain will safely keep these records and speed up the whole process removing any physical needs, manual methods or human factors.

The Fourth Stage

The final stage often involves the official announcement and declaration of election results to the public. This might seem like a straightforward phase but in reality, it can be complex, because it relates to the previous stage that involves how votes are secured, counted and recorded. The opponents of e-voting were mainly concerned about this stage due to the ease of temperament with data in the cyber environment and the lack of trust toward digital systems. However, as mentioned above, blockchain prevents this from happening.

In this stage, the app will show openly the recording of votes as well as surveys and opinions, and then immediately announce the results transparently to public. Access to information would be instant in a system like this. By creating servers and nodes at every level of electoral districts (rather than a national scale one), the system would work faster and without hindrance. That would help the results to be rapidly revealed to the people.

Table 7.2. Blockchain in Stages of E-Voting (Bulut et al., 2019: 4)

- *Authentication:*
  - ° Node gets *credentials ← (voter_id, password)* and sends them with its *node_id* to e-government system.
  - ° E-govemment system validates user credentials, *validate (credentials. node_id, usersInfo).*

- *Voting:*
  - ° Let vote be *v ← vote (voter_id, candidate)*
  - ° v is added to blockchain, *add (v, chain)*
  - ° chain information updated for all the voting machines
  - ° voter's related field is changed to voted in e-government system, *vote (voter_id, userList, true).*

- *Counting:*
  - ° Candidates are received from government, *candidates ← getCandidates(candidateList).*
  - ° Using highest level chain, votes are counted and winner of the regions are determined, *results ← count (chain, candidates).*
  - ° Final blockchain can be distributed to any third party to inspect the anonym votes with.

A perfectly secure electronic environment would mean greater transparency and accountability. It would mean access to national data by anyone, anytime that can lead to growth in analyses of long-term data and comparative frameworks not only in domestic politics and elections but also between states. In addition to electoral data other important information such as party statutes, party financial spreads, membership records, meeting minutes, etc. can be secured and accessed via blockchain technology.

In addition to voting for political parties, e-voting systems can be used to conduct a wide range of surveys and polls, allowing people to directly vote on specific issues, such as constitutional amendments, policy changes, major projects, opinion polls, market research, employee surveys, satisfaction questionnaires, organizational culture surveys, or let people join online deliberation and debate platforms (such as citizen forums, town hall meetings, and public hearings). Online deliberation has the potential to increase citizen engagement and foster more inclusive and deliberative forms of democratic decision making. Several studies have found that online deliberation can increase citizen engagement and foster more inclusive and deliberative forms of democratic decision making (Klein and Goldfarb, 2017; Andersen et al., 2012). However, other studies have found that online deliberation initiatives may be subject to the same biases and inequalities as traditional forms of political participation (Coleman and Moss, 2012). Additionally, it can encourage digital petitions—as a form of online political engagement, engaging citizens to express their opinions and preferences on a wide range of issues, increasing participation, political mobilization and influence political decision making. However, the impact of digital petitions on political decision making depends on several factors, including the size and composition of the petitioners, the salience of the issue, and the responsiveness of political elites. Several studies have found that digital petitions can influence political decision making, particularly when they are supported by a large and diverse group of signatories (Bimber et al., 2018; Leston-Bandeira et al., 2016).

Effects of AI Programming, Algorithms and Conclusions

Now with the developments in AI technologies and as they keep evolving, they will inevitably be added to the e-voting and blockchain systems, thus, completing the circle. Research on AI explores how it could be utilized to improve civic engagement, data analysis, and automated governance. Even though, questions remain about how AI decision making could be ensured to align with democratic values and ethical standards, it seems that it could be applied to many areas of contemporary political processes. AI could help parties formulating campaigns and advertisements; it can develop and enhance party or member discourses; it can be used to instantly translate speeches for different ethnic groups; it can help optimizing sampling for surveys or automating opinion polls, surveys and measurement of public opinion; it can be used to automatically develop reports on election results and compare or categorize them based on region, time or parties. AI can easily automate results and demographics while keeping anonymity and confidentiality. Combined with blockchain, the decentralized essence of these systems would prevent a monopoly to be established as is the case with social media corporations. Constant involvement of people and secured systems could eventually disengage internet trolls, manipulators, hackers, post-truth discourse, misinformation, and fake news; hence providing a foothold in countering right-wing populism, conservatism and xenophobia.

An e-voting scheme that utilizes a special software as described above, can alleviate many of the problems that emerge in current electoral systems. Not only it would establish faster, smoother, cheaper, cost-efficient, more secure and transparent elections that will not depend on human factors; but it will also implement direct and regular participation of people on most levels of decision and policy making, which could prevent elements of temporal rigidity, low levels of intra-party democracy, fusion of the executive, party centralization, hidden party finances or information, under-representation, moral hazard, choosing of wrong representatives, invalid votes, low levels of turnout, blocked voice phenomena. Constant interactions among people and representatives would also prevent agenda changing strategies, manipulation by demagogues/opportunists or fake discourses/news. It will open pathways to easier registration, distant voting, faster calculations, easy access to all sorts of data, statistics or demographics, user-friendly and easier to read adjustable visuals, improved efficiency, and healthier collection of data. On a broader scale, it would prevent attempts at authoritarianism.

Effects of a digital system that combines representatives with direct democratic principles that are utilized digitally can challenge elites, powerful lobbies (such as the oil lobby, cigarette companies, arms dealers, etc.), oligarchs, financially influential groups, businesses, international organizations, multinational corporations and companies, internet giants (amazon, google, meta, x, etc.). It can categorize public opinion based on how citizens score certain issues, on what the people demand, and analyze their comments. It gives the flexibility so that people who choose to be involved or interested in a subject can go into the details during their vote while others can only choose to have a simple vote. It could enable people to abstain from voting on issues they feel less informed about, while allowing them to show their knowledge level through additional questions or by scoring the issue's importance. This could be factored into vote counting for more nuanced results.

These systems, while securing against any fraud, can also take power or decision making burdens away from MPs and share to the representatives a more knowledgeable and detailed version of what people want and how important a particular policy is to them, better understanding of voter preferences. People that focus on a specific issue in a certain region could be better realized and different strategies and policies would be developed for specific areas. This would potentially benefit minorities or ethnic/religious groups. The disenchantment of the public that stemmed from the feeling of their vote not being able to make a change would be eliminated and echo chambers would be broken because everyone would have a chance in attending the process. In the long run, those with better knowledge on a particular issue would rise to prominence, breeding a more educated and aware platform for debate and shaping political culture. This would give a stronger sense of participation and effect on politics for the people, enhancing trust and legitimacy; provision of information, the facilitation of citizen participation, freedom of speech, voice, free-will, freedom of association and the use of technology to enhance transparency and accountability and overcome traditional barriers to political participation, such as geographical distance and physical disabilities. These designs not only apply to parliamentary or presidential elections, but it can be utilized on a multitude of areas ranging from elections for local administrations, municipalities, governors, executive boards, mayors, provinces, states, and finally referendums. They can also be adapted to work for parliamentary meeting notes, parliamentary votes on legislation and bills, primary elections of candidates within parties and other institutions.

Table 7.3. Hypothetical Types of E-Democracy and E-Voting Utilizing AI and Blockchain Systems

Regular E-Voting	**Participant E-Voting**
Public votes for candidates or parties and in some cases, referendums. Direct transition of regular electoral systems to digital world.	Public votes for candidates and parties but they are also involved in every stage of policy making. People vote on policies and issues as well.
Hybrid E-Voting	**Direct Democratic E-Voting**
Public votes for candidates and parties but they are also involved in every stage of policy making. There also extensive questionnaires and surveys on public opinion additionally in each vote.	Number of representatives are minimalized. Public is directly involved in every stage of decision making. Collective decision making and participation is maximized.

Therefore, the prospects for a direct democratic system are expanding with the evolution of technologies. This can vary from a standard transition of current systems to digital platforms; or to a more direct democracy hybrid where people can be involved in all levels of decision making by voting through their e-devices, attending referendums, issue initiatives, policymaking, surveys, opinion polls, etc. (Table 7.3). Even though it might take a long time for conservative and traditional systems to adopt them, eventually this is where the world will evolve toward. And it seems that the advantages of e-democracy are outweighing the disadvantages and ever more so than before.

Bibliography

Acharya, A. (1992). "Regional Military-Security Cooperation in the Third World: A Conceptual and Comparative Study of the Association of Southeast Asian Nations." *Journal of Peace Research*, 29 (1), 7–21.

Acharya, A. (2007). "The Emerging Regional Architecture of World Politics." *World Politics*. 59 (4), 629–652.

Acharya, A. (2010). "Asia is not One." *Journal of Asian Studies*. 69 (4), 1001–1013.

Acharya, A. (2014). "Call for Proposals: Global IR and Regional Worlds, A New Agenda for International Studies." *International Studies Quarterly*, 54 (4), 647–659.

Acharya, A.(2018a). *The End of American World Order*. Cambridge: Polity Press.

Acharya, A. (2018b). *Constructing Global Order: Agency and Change in World Politics*. Cambridge: Cambridge University Press.).

Ádám, Z. (2023). Economic Versus Authoritarian: Economic and Social Policies of Alternating Populisms in Pre- and Post-2010 Hungary. In J. Chacko Chennattuserry, M. Deshpande, & P. Hong (Eds.), Encyclopedia of New Populism and Responses in the 21st Century (pp. 1–10). Springer Nature. <https://doi.org/10.1007/978-981-16-9859-0_11-1>

Aguiar, P. (2017). Who Owns the Media in Brazil?

Ahmad, M., Rehman, A. U., Ayub, N., Alshehri, M. D., Khan, M. A., Hameed, A., & Yetgin, H. (2020). Security, Usability, and Biometric Authentication Scheme for Electronic Voting using Multiple Keys. International Journal of Distributed Sensor Networks, 16(7).

Ahuja, M. K., Galletta, D. F., & Carley, K. M. (2003). Individual Centrality and Performance in Virtual R&D Groups: An Empirical Study. Management Science, 49(1), 21–38. <https://doi.org/10.1287/mnsc.49.1.21.12756>

Alden, E., & Schurmann, F. (1992). Neo-Nationalist Fallacies. *Foreign Policy* (87), pp. 105–122.

Al-Marashi, I. & Causevic, A. (2020). NATO and collective environmental security in the MENA: From the Cold War to Covid-19. *Journal of Strategic Security*, 13(4), 28–44.

Alvarez, R. MM., & Hall, T. (2008). *Electronic Elections: The Perils and Promises of Digital Democracy*. Princeton University Press, NJ.

Alvarez, R. M., Hall, T. & Llewellyn, M. (2008). Are Americans Confident Their Ballots Are Counted? *Journal of Politics*, 70(3), 754–766.

Amin, S. (1999). "Regionalization in Response to Polarizing Globalization" In Hettne, Björn, Andras Inotai ve Osvaldo Sunkel (eds.). *Globalism and the New Regionalism* (pp.54–84). London: Palgrave Macmillan.

Analiza—"Otvoreni Balkan" se može pokazati kao loša ideja, Anadolu Agency. Retrieved from: <https://www.aa.com.tr/ba/analiza-vijesti/analiza-otvoreni-balkan-se-mo%C5%BEepokazati-kao-lo%C5%A1a-ideja/2618782, 26.04.2024>.

Anderson, B. (2007). *Hayali Cemaatler: Milliyetçiliğin Kökenleri ve Yayılması* (4. Basım ed.). İstanbul: Metis Yayıncılık.

Atkeson, L. R., & Saunders, K. L. (2007). The Effect of Election Administration on Voter Confidence: A Local Matter? *PS: Political Science and Politics*, 40(4), 655–660.

Avgerou, C., Ganzaroli, A., Poulymenakou, A., & Reinhard, N. (2009). Interpreting the Trustworthiness of Government Mediated by Information and Communication Technology: Lessons from Electronic Voting in Brazil. *Information Technology for Development*, 15(2), 133–148.

Aydın-Düzgit, S. (2020). Can non-democracies support international democracy? Turkey as a case study. Third World Quarterly, 41(2), 264–283. <https://doi.org/10.1080/01436597.2019.1636643>

Bagdikıan, B. H. (2004). The New Media monopoly. Beacon press.

Baker, C. E. (2006). Media Concentration and Democracy: Why Ownership Matters (1st ed.). Cambridge University Press. <https://doi.org/10.1017/CBO9780511810992>

Banerjee, S. (2005). Pitfalls of Neo-nationalism. *Economic and Political Weekly, 40*(33), 3629–3631.

Bangstad, S. (2015). The racism that dares not speak its name: Rethinking neo-nationalism and neo-racism in Norway. *Intersections. East European Journal of Society and Politics, 1*(1), 49–65.

Bánkuti, M., Halmai, G., & Scheppele, K. L. (2012). Disabling the Constitution. Journal of Democracy, 23(3), 138–146. <https://doi.org/10.1353/jod.2012.0054>

Bardi, L., Bartolini, S., & Trechsel, A. (2014). Party adaptation and change and the crisis of democracy. Party Politics, 20(2), 151–159. <https://doi.org/10.1177/1354068813519966>

Bátorfy, A., & Urbán, Á. (2020). State advertising as an instrument of transformation of the media market in Hungary. East European Politics, 36(1), 44–65. <https://doi.org/10.1080/21599165.2019.1662398>

Batory, A. (2022). More Power, Less Support: The Fidesz Government and the Coronavirus Pandemic in Hungary. Government and Opposition, 1–17. <https://doi.org/10.1017/gov.2022.3>

Beaudet, P. (1993). Crisis of Nationalism: Back to the Future. *Economic and Political Weekly*, 2648–2649.

Beaulieu, E. (2016). Electronic Voting and Perceptions of Election Fraud and Fairness. Journal of Experimental Political Science, 3, 18–31.

Beeson, Mark and Philomena Murray (2020). "Testing Times for Regionalism: Coping with Great Power Rivalry in the Asia-Pacific." *Asian Studies Review*, 44 (1), 1–9.

Belder, F. (2023). The politics of populism in Hungary: By Robert Csehi, Abingdon, UK and New York, USA, Routledge Studies in Democratic Crisis, 2022, 242pp., £130.00 (hardback), ISBN: 978036747686; £38.99 (paperback), ISBN: 9781032075679; £27.29 (EBook), ISBN: 9781003035862. Eurasian Geography and Economics, 0(0), 1–2. <https://doi.org/10.1080/15387216.2023.2222759>.

Bell, C. (2024). *PeaceTech: Digital Transformation to End Wars*. Cham, Switzerland: Palgrave Macmillan.

Bennett, A. (2023). Polarization & populist backlash in transitioning Tunisia: The role of internet media & media ownership. British Journal of Middle Eastern Studies, 0(0), 1–23. <https://doi.org/10.1080/13530194.2023.2230151>

Bennett, T. (1983). Culture, Society and the Media. Contemporary Sociology. <https://www.academia.edu/47140191/Culture_Society_and_the_Media>

Benvenuto, S., Howarth, D., & Norval, A. (2012). On Populist Reason by Ernesto Laclau. 633–646.

Berezin, M. (2002). Secure states: toward a political sociology of emotion. *The Sociological Review*, 50(2), 33–52.

Bergmann, E. (2020). *Neo-nationalism: The rise of nativist populism.* Cham: Springer Nature.

Berntzen, L. E. (2020). How Elite Politicization of Terror Impacts Sympathies for Partisans: Radical Right versus Social Democrats. Politics and Governance, 8(3), 19–31. <https://doi.org/10.17645/pag.v8i3.2919>

Best, E., Thomas C. (2016). "Regionalism in International Affairs" In Baylis, John, Steve Smith ve Patricia Owens (eds.), *The Globalization of World Politics* (pp. 1–22). Oxford: Oxford University Press.

Bieber, F. (2018). Is nationalism on the rise? Assessing global trends. *Ethnopolitics, 17*(5), pp. 519–540.

Bienenstock, E. J., & Bonacich, P. (2022). Eigenvector centralization as a measure of structural bias in information aggregation. The Journal of Mathematical Sociology, 46(3), 227–245. <https://doi.org/10.1080/0022250X.2021.1878357>

Bimber, B., Feldman, L., Wojcieszak, M., & Stroud, N. J. (2018). Explaining Media Choice: The Role of Issue-Specific Engagement in Predicting Interest-Based and Partisan Selectivity. Journal of Broadcasting & Electronic Media, 62(1), 109–130.

Birkinbine, B., Gómez García, R., & Wasko, J. (2016). Global Media Giants.

Birkinbine, B. J., & Gómez, R. (2020). New methods for mapping media concentration: Network analysis of joint ventures among firms. Media, Culture & Society, 42(7–8), 1078–1094. <https://doi.org/10.1177/0163443720902907>

Bithymitris, G. (2017). Socio-cultural Aspects of Neo-nationalism in Crisis Contexts. *Acta Politologica*, 9(1), pp. 61–74.

Bjånesøy, L. (2023). Negative partisanship and the populist radical right: The case of Norway. Scandinavian Political Studies, 46(1–2), 99–120. <https://doi.org/10.1111/1467-9477.12247>

Bonacich, P. (2007). Some unique properties of eigenvector centrality. Social Networks, 29(4), 555–564. <https://doi.org/10.1016/j.socnet.2007.04.002>

Bowler, S., & Donovan, T. (2016). *Designing Digital Democracy.* Cambridge University Press.

Boylan, B. M. (2015). In pursuit of independence: the political economy of Catalonia's secessionist movement. *Nations and nationalism, 21*(4), 761–785.

Boylan, B., McBeath, J., & Wang, B. (2021). US-China relations: Nationalism, the trade war, and COVID-19. *Fudan Journal of the Humanities and Social Sciences, 14*(1), 23–4.

Börzel, T. A., Thomas R. (2016). "Introduction: Framework of the Handbook and Conceptual Clarifications" In Börzel, Tanja A. ve Thomas Risse (eds.). *The Oxford Handbook of Comparative Regionalism* (pp. 3–15). Oxford: Oxford University Press.

Breuilly, J. (2005). Nationalism and the State. In P. Spencer, & H. Wollman, *Netions and Nationalism: A Reader* (pp. 61–73). Edinburgh: Edinburgh University Press.

Brubaker, R. (2017a). Why populism? *Theory and society, 46*, pp. 357–385.

Brubaker, R. (2017b). Between nationalism and civilizationism: The European populist moment in comparative perspective. *Ethnic and Racial Studies, 40*(8), pp. 1191–1226.

Bruff, I. (2014). The Rise of Authoritarian Neoliberalism. Rethinking Marxism, 26(1), 113–129. <https://doi.org/10.1080/08935696.2013.843250>

Bugaric, B. (2019). The two faces of populism: Between authoritarian and democratic populism. German Law Journal, 20(3), 390–400. <https://doi.org/10.1017/glj.2019.20>

Buğra, A. (2009). "Polanyi'nin Çifte Hareket Kavramı ve Günümüz Piyasa Toplumunda Siyaset" In Buğra, Ayşe ve Kaan Ağartan (eds.), *21 Yüzyılda Karl Polanyi'yi Okumak: Bir Siyasi Proje Olarak Piyasa Ekonomisi* (pp.237–260). İstanbul: İletişim.

Bullock, C. S., Hood, M. V., & Clark, R. (2005). Punch Cards, Jim Crow, and Al Gore: Explaining Voter Trust in the Electoral System in Georgia, 2000. State Politics and Policy Quarterly, 5(3), 283–94.

Bulut, R., Kantarci, A., Keskin, S. & Bahtiyar, Ş. (2019). Blockchain-Based Electronic Voting System for Elections in Turkey. Paper presented at (UBMK'19) 4th International Conference on Computer Science and Engineering, 183, 11–15.

Bund, J. (2016). *Cybersecurity and Democracy: Hacking, Leaking, and Voting.* European Union Institute for Security Studies.

Busek, E., Kühne, B. (2010). *From Stabilization to Integration: The Stability Pact for Southe Eastern Europe*. Wien: Bohlau Verlag.

Byrne, M. D. (2017). Improving Voting Systems' User-Friendliness, Reliability, & Security. *Behavioral Science & Policy*, 3(1), 1–9.

Callahan, W. A. (2003). Beyond Cosmopolitanism and Nationalism: Diasporic Chinese and Neo-nationalism in China and Thailand. *International Organization*, 57(3), 481–517.

Campbell, B. A., Tossell, C. C., Byrne, M. D., & Kortum, P. (2014). Toward More Usable Electronic Voting: Testing the Usability of a Smartphone Voting System. *Human Factors*, 56(5), 973–985.

Card, D., & Moretti, E. (2007). Does Voting Technology Affect Election Outcomes? Touch-Screen Voting and the 2004 Presidential Election. *Review of Economics and Statistics*, 89, 660–673.

Carr, E. H. (1945). *Nationalism and after.* Macmillan.

Castels, S. (2005). Citizenship and the Other in the Age of Migration. In P. Spencer, & H. Wollman, *Nations and Nationalism* (pp. 301–316). Edinburgh: Edinburgh University Press.

Causevic, A. & Al-Marashi, I. (2023). *Connections QJ*, 22(1), 67–78.

Celeste, R., Thornburgh, D. & Lin, H. (eds.). (2006). *Asking the Right Questions About Electronic Voting*. The National Academies Press, Washington DC.

Chang, C. C., & Lee, J. S. (2006). An Anonymous and Flexible í-out-of-n Electronic Voting Scheme. *Journal of Discrete Mathematical Sciences and Cryptography*, 9(1), 133–151.

Changfoot, N., & Cullen, B. (2011). Why is Quebec separatism off the agenda? Reducing national unity crisis in the neoliberal era. *Canadian Journal of Political Science/Revue canadienne de science politique*, 44(4), 769–787.

Chatterjee, P. (2005). Whose Imagined Community? In P. Spencer, & H. Wollman, *Nations and Nationalism* (pp. 237–247). Edinburgh: Edinburgh University Press.

Chen, G., & Wang, X. (2022). Online political incivility in YouTube comments during the 2020 US presidential election. Computers in Human Behavior, <https://doi.org/10.1016/j.chb.2022.107028>

Chesterley, N., & Roberti, P. (2018). Populism and institutional capture. European Journal of Political Economy, 53, 1–12. <https://doi.org/10.1016/j.ejpoleco.2017.06.004>

Chung, Y. F., & Wu, Z. Y. (2012). Casting Ballots over Internet Connection Against Bribery and Coercion. *The Computer Journal*, 55(10), 118–122.

Claassen, R. L., Magleby, D. B., Monson, J. Q., & Patterson, K. D. (2013). Voter Confidence and the Election-Day Voting Experience. Political Behavior, 35, 215–35.

Clowes, E. (2020). Notorious Neo-Nationalism: A Cultural-Studies Reading of Post-Imperial Anxiety,

Coleman, S., & Blumler, J. G. (2009). *The Future of Democracy: Can Technology Strengthen Democracy?* Cambridge University Press.

Coleman, S., & Shane, P. (2012). *The Internet and Democratic Citizenship: Theory, Practice and Policy*. Cambridge University Press.

Cormack, C. B. (2016). Why Use Electronic Voting? Report Title: Democracy Rebooted. Atlantic Council.

Crna Gora trenutno nije zainteresovana za Otvoreni Balkan: Prioritet zajedničko tržište pod okriljem EU, Retrieved from: <https://www.vijesti.me/vijesti/politika/562428/crnagora-trenutno-nije-zainteresovana-za-otvoreni-balkan-prioritet-zajednicko-trziste-podokriljem-eu, 119.04.2024>.

Cross, R., & Cummings, J. N. (2004). Tie and Network Correlates of Individual Performance in Knowledge-Intensive Work. The Academy of Management Journal, 47(6), 928–937. <https://doi.org/10.2307/20159632>

Cyber-Warfare, and Russia's Return to Authoritarianism. *New Area Studies*, 1(1), pp. 41–72.

Çağlak, E., & Pekcan, G. E. (2022). Politik Gündemi Takip Aracı Olarak Youtube: Babala TV Örneği. *Kültür Araştırmaları Dergisi*, (13), 275–294.

Dahlgren, P. (2013). *The political web: Media, participation and alternative democracy*. Palgrave Macmillan.

"Da li je Otvoreni Balkan prečica do EU?," Danas, August 16, 2022. Retrieved from: <https://www.danas.rs/vesti/politika/demostat/da-li-je-otvorenibalkan-precica-do-eu/,19.04.2024>.

Davis, L., & Deole, S. (2017). Immigration and the rise of far-right parties in Europe. *ifo DICE Report, 15*(4), 10–15.

Davletov, B., Kalkar U., Ragnet, M. & Verhulst, S. (2022, November). Peacetech topic map: A research base for an emerging field. Retrieved June 22, 2024, from https://files.thegovlab.org/PeaceTechTopicMap.pdf

DeCoste, F. (1995). Persons/Peoples/Polity: Interrogating Neonationalism in Quebec. *Review of Constitutional Studies, 4*(2), 290–347.

De Filippi, P., & Wright, A. (2018). Blockchain and Public Choice: Can Blockchain Revolutionize Voting? *Harvard Journal of Law & Technology, 31*(1), 165–206.

De Lange, S. L. (2016). A new winning formula? The programmatic appeal of the radical right. In C. Mudde, *The populist radical right: A reader* (pp. 101–120). London: Routledge.

Delwit, P., Kulahci, E. & Pilet, J. B. (2005). Electronic Voting in Belgium: A Legitimized Choice? *Politics, 25*(3), 153–164.

Desai, Z., & Lee, A. (2021). Technology and protest: the political effects of electronic voting in India. Political Science Research and Methods, 9, 398–413.

Devanesan, V. V., & Chandrasekaran, P. K. A. (2011). E-Democracy in India: Implications and Imperatives. The Indian Journal of Political Science, 72(2), 395–401.

Diamond, L. (2015). Facing Up to the Democratic Recession. Journal of Democracy, 26(1), 141–155.

Dodik: Džaferović i Komšić ponovo odbili da podrže Otvoreni Balkan, Politika. Retrieved from: <https://www.politika.rs/sr/clanak/512709/Dodik-Dzaferovic-i-Komsic-ponovo-odbilida-podrze-Otvoreni-Balkan>, 24.04.2024.

Doroshenko, L. (2018). Far-Right Parties in the European Union and Media Populism: A Comparative Analysis of 10 Countries During European Parliament Elections. International Journal of Communication, 12(0), Article 0. <https://ijoc.org/index.php/ijoc/article/view/7757>

Down, I., & Han, K. (2021). Far-right parties and "Europe": societal polarization and the limits of EU issue contestation. *Journal of European Integration, 43*(1), 65–81.

Drescher, D. (2017). *Blockchain Basics: A Non-Technical Introduction in 25 Steps*. Apress, Frankfurt.

Đukanović D. (2022). "The Open Balkan: Challenges of Sustainability and Unfinished Inclusion," Report on regional integration 'Open Balkans'." Igman Initiative, retrieved from: <https://www.igmaninitiative. org/wpcontent/uploads/2022/06/IZVESTAJ-OPENBALKAN-PDF.pdf>, 23.04.2024.

Đukanović, D. (2020). *Balkan na posthladnoratovskom raskršću (1989–2020)*. Beograd: Službeni glasnik.

Đukanović, D., Antevski, M. (2008). "Razlike između stare i nove CEFTA," Stojić-Karanović (eds). *Centralnoevropska zona slobodne trgovine i interesi Srbije*, Belgrade: Institut za međunarodnu politiku i privredu.

Đukanović, D., Dasić, M. (2021). "Modeliranje regionalne saradnje na Balkanu nakon 1999. godine: evropska iskustva i njihova primena". *Međunarodni problemi*. DOI <https://doi.org/10.2298/MEDJP2104617D>. 4, pp. 617–636.

Đukanović, D., Đorđević, B. (2020). "'Mali Šengen'—koncept, implementacija i kontroverze". *Međunarodni problemi*. DOI: <https://doi.org/10.2298/MEDJP2003595D>. 3, pp. 595–618.

Dunn, J. (1999). Nationalism. In R. Beiner, *Theorizing Nationalism* (pp. 27–50). New York: SUNY Press.

Duroy, Q. (2020). The Rise of Neo-Nationalism in Europe: A Veblenian Perspective. *Journal of Economic Issues, 54*(4), pp. 987–1001.

Duroy, Q. (n.d.). National Identity and Structural Incompatibilities: On the Rise of Neo-nationalism in Europe.

Dursun, D. (2018) Siyaset Bilimi, Eskişehir: Anadolu Üniversitesi Açıköğretim Fakültesi Yayınları.

Eaksittipong, S. (2021). The Chinese of Thailand: Academic Diplomacy and the Convergence of Sino-Thai Intellectual Nationalisms. In C.-Y. Hoon, & Y.-k. Chan, *Contesting Chineseness: Ethnicity, Identity, and Nation in China and Southeast Asia* (pp. 101–122). Singapore: Springer.

Earle, J. S., Kucsera, C., & Telegdy, Á. (2005). Ownership Concentration and Corporate Performance on the Budapest Stock Exchange: Do too many cooks spoil the goulash? Corporate Governance:

An International Review, 13(2), 254–264. <https://doi.org/10.1111/j.1467-8683.2005.00420.x>

Eger, M. A., & Valdez, S. (2014). Neo-nationalism in Western Europe. *European Sociological Review*, 1–16.

Eger, M. A., & Valdez, S. (2019). From radical right to neo-nationalist. *European Political Science, 18*, pp. 379–399.

Elçi, E. (2019). The Rise of Populism in Turkey: A Content Analysis. Southeast European and Black Sea Studies, 19(3), 387–408. <https://doi.org/10.1080/14683857.2019.1656875>

Esen, B., & Gumuscu, S. (2018). Building a competitive authoritarian regime: State–business relations in the AKP's Turkey. Journal of Balkan and Near Eastern Studies, 20(4), 349–372. <https://doi.org/10.1080/19448953.2018.1385924>

Esser, F., Aalberg, T., & Stępińska, Agnieszka. (2017). Populism and social media: How politicians spread a fragmented ideology. Information Communication and Society, 20(8), 1109–1126. <https://doi.org/10.1080/1369118X.2016.1207697>

Fawcett, L. (2004). "Exploring Regional Domains: A Comparative History of Regionalism." *International Affairs*. 80 (3), 429–446.

Fawcett, L. (2005). "The Origins and Development of Regional Ideas in the Americas" In Fawcett, Louise ve Monica Serrano (eds.), *Regionalism and Governance in the Americas* (pp.27–51). New York: Palgrave Macmillan.

Fawcett, L. (2017). "Regions and Regionalism" In Beeson, Mark ve Nick Bisley (eds.), *Issues in 21st Century World Politics* (pp. 97–112). New York: Palgrave Macmillan.

Figenschou, T. U., & Beyer, A. (2014). The Limits of the Debate: How the Oslo Terror Shook the Norwegian Immigration Debate. The International Journal of Press/Politics, 19(4), 430–452. <https://doi.org/10.1177/1940161214542954>

Freedman, D. (2018). Populism and media policy failure. European Journal of Communication, 33(6), 604–618. <https://doi.org/10.1177/0267323118790156>

Freedman, D. (2021). Media policy failures and the emergence of right-wing populism. In H. Tumber & S. Waisbord (Eds.), The Routledge

Companion to Media Disinformation and Populism (1st ed., pp. 411–419). Routledge. <https://doi.org/10.4324/9781003004431-43>

Freedom House. (2023). Hungary: Freedom in the World 2023 Country Report. Freedom House. <https://freedomhouse.org/country/hungary/freedom-world/2023>

Fuchs, C. (2018). Authoritarian capitalism, authoritarian movements and authoritarian communication. Media, Culture & Society, 40(5), 779–791. <https://doi.org/10.1177/0163443718772147>

Galetić, F., Dabić, M., & Kiessling, T. (2016). Media Control: A Case for Privatization in Transitional Economies. Journal of Media Economics, 29(3), 111–124. <https://doi.org/10.1080/08997764.2016.1206907>

Galtung, J. & Fischer, D. (2013). *Johan Galtung*, SpringerBriefs on Pioneers in Science and Practice 5.

Gao, M. (2012). The rise of neo-nationalism and the New Left: A postcolonial and postmodern perspective. In L. Liew, & S. Wang, *Nationalism, democracy and national integration in China* (pp. 44–62). London: Routledge.

Gates, M. (2017). Blockchain: Ultimate Guide. Wise Fox Publishing.

Gerbaudo, P. (2012). *Technopolitics and Protest: New Media Activism in the Arab Spring.* Pluto Press.

Gilens, M., & Hertzman, C. (2000). Corporate Ownership and News Bias: Newspaper Coverage of the 1996 Telecommunications Act. The Journal of Politics, 62(2), 369–386. <https://doi.org/10.1111/0022-3816.00017>

Gingrich, A. (2006). Neo-nationalism and the Reconfiguration of Europe. *Social Anthropology, 14*(2), 195–217.

Gingrich, A., & Banks, M. (2006). Introduction. In A. Gingrich, & M. Banks, *Neo-nationalism in Europe and beyond: perspectives from social anthropology* (pp. 1–26). Berghahn Books.

Glybchenko, Y. (2024). Virtual reality technologies as PeaceTech: Supporting Ukraine in practice and research. *Journal of Peacebuilding & Development, 19*(1), 117–122.

Golder, M. (2003). Explaining Variation in the Success of Extreme Right Parties in Western Europe. *Comparative Political Studies, 36*(4), 432–466.

Golder, M. (2016). Far-right parties in Europe. *Annual review of political science, 19*(1), 477–497.

Greenfeld, L. (1994). *Nationalism: Five Roads to Modernity* (2. ed.). Cambridge: Harward University Press.

Gümrükçü, S. B. (2022). Populist discourse, (counter-)mobilizations and democratic backsliding in Turkey. Turkish Studies, 23(3), 407–429. <https://doi.org/10.1080/14683849.2021.1999814>

Güngör, S. (2017). Siyasetin @ hali: Dijital çağda siyasal katılım. Süleyman Demirel Üniversitesi İktisadi ve İdari Bilimler Fakültesi Dergisi, 22, p. 2259–2273.

Hacker, K. L., & van Dijk, J. A. G. M. (Eds.). (2000). Digital Democracy: Issues of Theory and Practice. SAGE Publications.

Hall, T. (2012). Electronic Voting. In Electronic Democracy by Kersting, N., Stein, M., & Trent, J. (eds.). Verlag Barbara Budrich.

Halperin, S. (2018). "Polanyi's Two Transformations Revisited: A 'Bottom Up' Perspective." *Globalizations.* 15 (7), 911–923.

Hamilton, J. T. (2007). Media Concentration and Democracy: Why Ownership Matters, by C. Edwin Baker Fighting for Air: The Battle to Control America's Media, by Eric Klinenberg: Cambridge, England: Cambridge University Press, 2007. 272 pp. $65.00 cloth; $22.99 paper New York: Metropolitan Books, 2007. 352 pp. $26.00 cloth; $16.00 paper. Political Communication, 24(4), 455–457. <https://doi.org/10.1080/10584600701641664>.

Hanretty, C. (2014). Media outlets and their moguls: Why concentrated individual or family ownership is bad for editorial independence. European Journal of Communication, 29(3), 335–350. <https://doi.org/10.1177/0267323114523150>

Harrison, S., & Bruter, M. (2011). *Mapping extreme right ideology: an empirical geography of the European extreme right.* Hampshire: Palgrave Macmillan.

Hasen, R. L. (2005). Beyond the Margin of Litigation: Reforming US Election Administration to Avoid Electoral Meltdown. *Washington and Lee Law Review,* 62(3), 937–999.

Haynes, J. (2021). *Trump and the politics of neo-nationalism: The Christian Right and secular nationalism in America.* London: Taylor & Francis.

Hearn, J. (2002). Identity, Class and Civil Society in Scotland's Neo-nationalism. *Nations and Nationalism, 8*(1), 15–30.

Heller, R. (2018). Defending Social Status–Why Russia's Ukraine Policy is About More than Regional Leadership. *Rising Powers Quarterly, 2*(1), 137–159.

Hellmann, O. (2021). The dictator's screenplay: Collective memory narratives and the legitimacy of communist rule in East Asia. Democratization, 28(4), 659–683. <https://doi.org/10.1080/13510347.2020.1849146>

Hellmeier, S., Cole, R., Grahn, S., Kolvani, P., Lachapelle, J., Lührmann, A., Maerz, S. F., Pillai, S., & Lindberg, S. I. (2021). State of the World 2020: Autocratization Turns Viral. Democratization, 28(6), 1053–1074.

Hellström, A., & Nilsson, T. (2008, Nisan). *<http://dspace.mah.se>*. Retrieved Aralık 23, 2015 from Malmö University: <http://dspace.mah.se:8080/bitstream/handle/2043/7145/We%20are%20the%20Good%20Guys.pdf?sequence=1&isAllowed=y>

Herrnson, P. S., Bederson, B. B., Lee, B., Francia, P. L., Sherman, R. M., Conrad, F. G., Traugott, M., & Niemi, R. G. (2005). Early Appraisals of Electronic Voting. *Social Science Computer Review*, 23(3), 274–292.

Herrnson, P. S., Niemi, R. G., Hanmer, M. J., Francia, P. L., Bederson, B. B., Conrad, F. G., & Traugott, M. W. (2008).

Herron, M. C., & Wand, J. (2007). Assessing Partisan Bias in Voting Technology: The Case of the 2004 New Hampshire Recount. *Electoral Studies*, 26, 247–261.

Hervik, P. (2011). *The Annoying Difference: The Emergence of Danish Neonationalism, Neoracism, and Populism in the Post-1989 World*. New York: Berghahn Books.

Hervik, P. (2020). Neo-nationalism and far-right studies: Anthropological perspectives. In S. Ashe, J. Busher, G. Macklin, & A. Winter, *Researching the Far Right* (pp. 92–108). London: Routledge.

Hettne, B. (1993). "Neo-Mercantilism: The Pursuit of Regionness." *Cooperation and Conflict*. 28 (3). Pp. 211–232.

Hettne, B. (1999). "Globalization and the New Regionalism: The Second Great Transformation" In Hettne, Björn, Andras Inotai ve Osvaldo Sunkel (eds.), *Globalism and the New Regionalism* (pp1–24). London: Palgrave Macmillan.

Hettne, B. (2003). "The New Regionalism Revisited" In Söderbaum, Fredrik ve Timothy M. Shaw (eds.), *Theories of New Regionalism: a Palgrave Reader* (pp.22–42). New York: Palgrave Macmillan.

Hettne, B. (2005). "Beyond the 'New' Regionalism," *New Political Economy.* 10 (4), pp. 543–571.

Hettne, B. (2008). "Teori ve Pratikte Güvenliğin Bölgeselleşmesi." (Trans. Evren Çelik Wiltse), *Uluslararası İlişkiler.* 5 (18), pp. 87–106.

Hettne, B. (2009). *Thinking About Development.* New York: Zed Books.

Heywood, A. (2019). *Küresel Siyaset*, Nasuh Uslu ve Haluk Özdemir trans. Ankara: Felix Kitap.

Hobsbawm, E. J. (1999). Ethnicity and Nationalism in Europe Today. G. Balakrishnan içinde, *Mapping the Nation* (s. 255–266). London: Varso.

Hobsbawm, E. J., & Kertzer, D. J. (1992). Ethnicity and nationalism in Europe today. *Anthropology today, 8*(1), 3–8.

Horáková, N. (2019). Neo-nationalism in the Czech Republic and its Self-Presentation on Social networks Using the example of Facebook. *Politeja, 61*, pp. 11–130.

Hoy, C. J. (1971). Electronic Voting. *American Libraries*, 2(2), 148–149.

Höyer, S. (1968). The Political Economy of the Norwegian Press*. Scandinavian Political Studies, 3(A3), 85–143. <https://doi.org/10.1111/j.1467-9477.1968.tb00460.x>

Hsiao, T. C., Wu, Z. Y., Liu, C. H., & Chung, Y. F. (2017). Electronic Voting Systems for Defending Free-will and Resisting Bribery and Coercion based on Ring Anonymous Signcryption Scheme. Advances in Mechanical Engineering, 9(1), 1–9.

Hughes, S., & Vorobyeva, Y. (2021). Explaining the killing of journalists in the contemporary era: The importance of hybrid regimes and subnational variations. Journalism, 22(8), 1873–1891. <https://doi.org/10.1177/1464884919885588>

Hurrell, A.(1995a), "Explaining the Resurgence of Regionalism in World Politics." *Review of International Studies.*21 (4), 331–358.

Hurrell, A. (1995b). "Regionalism in Theoretical Perspective" In Fawcett, Louise ve Andrew Hurrell (eds.), *Regionalism in World Politics* (pp. 37–73). New York: Oxford University Press.

Iacobucci, D., McBride, R., Popovich, D. L., & Rouziou, M. (2018). In Social Network Analysis, Which Centrality Index Should I Use?: Theoretical Differences and Empirical Similarities among Top Centralities. Journal of Methods and Measurement in the Social Sciences, 8(2), Article 2. <https://doi.org/10.2458/v8i2.22991>

Iansiti, M., & Lakhani, K. R. (2017). The Truth About Blockchain. Harvard Businness Review.

Ignazi, P. (2003). *Extreme right parties in Western Europe.* Oxford: Oxford University Press.

Ilić, D. (2021). "Šta je nama srpski svet?," *Peščanik*, retrieved from: <https://pescanik.net/sta-je-nama-srpski-svet/. 13.04.2024>.

Inghammar, A., & Skjønberg, A. S. (2023). The Impact of Populism on Scandinavian Labor Law: The Cases of Norway and Sweden. International Journal of Comparative Labor Law and Industrial Relations, 39(1). <https://kluwerlawonline.com/api/Product/CitationPDFURL?file=Journals\IJCL\IJCL2023006.pdf>

Ivarsflaten, E. (2008). What unites right-wing populists in Western Europe? Re-examining grievance mobilization models in seven successful cases. *Comparative Political Studies, 41*(1), 3–23.

Jamieson, K. H., Cappella, J. N., Jamieson, K. H., & Cappella, J. N. (2010). Echo Chamber: Rush Limbaugh and the Conservative Media Establishment. Oxford University Press.

Jansen, R. S. (2011). Populist mobilization: A new theoretical approach to populism. *Sociological theory, 29*(2), pp. 75–96.

Jefferson, D. R. (2007). E-democracy: Concepts and Practices. University Press of America.

Jenkins, H., & Thorburn, D. (Eds.). (2003). *Democracy and New Media.* MIT Press.

Johnson, D. W. (2004). Rethinking Electronic Voting. *Journal of Political Marketing*, 3(3), 107–109.

Joint Declaration by the President of the Republic of Serbia, Prime Minister of the Republic of Albania and the Prime Minister of the Republic North Macedonia on Implementing the EU Four Freedoms in the Western Balkans, retrieved from: <https://api.pks.rs/storage/assets/Deklaracija_Novi_Sad1.pdf>, 23.04.2024.

Joppke, C. (2021). Immigration Policy in the Crossfire of Neoliberalism and Neonationalism. *wiss Journal of Sociology, 47*(1), pp. 71–92.

Josifides, P. (1997). Methods of measuring media concentration. Media, Culture & Society, 19(4), 643–663. <https://doi.org/10.1177/016344397019004008>

Jovićević M.., (2021). "Popov: Ne idu 'srpski svet' i 'Otvoreni Balkan' zajedno," Pobjeda. Retrieved from: <https://www.pobjeda.me/clanak/ne-idu-srpski-svet-i-otvoreni-balkan-zajedno>. 13.04.2024.

Judis, J. B. (2001). Punch Drunk. *The American Prospect*, 12(5), 12–26.

Kalogeropoulos, A., et al. (2017). Who shares and comments on news? A cross-national comparative analysis of online and social media participation. Digital Journalism, 5(2), p. 177–200.

Kapferer, B., & Morris, B. (2006). Nationalism and Neo-populism in Australia. In A. Gingrich, & M. Banks, *Neo-nationalism in Europe and Beyond: Perspectives from Social Anthropology* (pp. 248–270). Berghahn Books.

Karadimitriou, A., von Krogh, T., Ruggiero, C., Biancalana, C., Bomba, M., & Lo, W. H. (2022). Investigative journalism and the watchdog role of news media: Between acute challenges and exceptional counterbalances. Nordicom, University of Gothenburg. <https://doi.org/10.48335/9789188855589-5>

Karataşlı, Ş. S., & Kumral, Ş. (2023). Crisis of capitalism and cycles of right-wing populism in contemporary Turkey: The making and unmaking of Erdoğanist hegemony. Journal of Agrarian Change, 23(1), 22–46. <https://doi.org/10.1111/joac.12501>

Katz, G., Alvarez, R. M., Calvo, E., Escolar, M., & Pomares, J. (2011). Assessing the Impact of Alternative Voting Technologies on Multi-Party Elections: Design Features, Heuristic Processing, and Voter Choice. *Political Behavior*, 33, 247–270.

Katzenstein, P. J. (2005). *A World of Regions: Asia and Europe in the American Imperium*. Ithaca: Cornell University Press.

Kemper, T. (2001). A structural approach to social movement emotions. In J. Goodwin, J. Jasper, & F. Polletta, *Passionate Politics: Emotions and Social Movements* (pp. 56–73). Chicago: University of Chicago Press.

Kenez, P. (1992). Nationalism on the Rise in Hungary. *The New Leader*, *75*(12), 1–5.

Kersten, R. (1999). Neo-nationalism and the "liberal school of history." *Japan Forum*, *11*(2), 191–203.

Kersting, N., & Baldersheim, H. (eds.) (2004). Electronic Voting and Democracy: A Comparative Analysis. Palgrave Macmillan.

Kersting, N., Stein, M., & Trent, J. (2012). *Electronic Democracy*. Verlag Barbara Budrich.

Kfir, I. (2015). NATO's paradigm shift: Searching for a traditional security–human security nexus, *Contemporary Security Policy*, *36*(2), 219–243.

Kher, M. (2015). The Electronic Voting Machine: A Continuous Process of Achieving Quality. *African Journal of Science, Technology, Innovation and Development*, *7*(2), 116–121.

Kiayias, A., & Lazos, P. (2022). SoK: Blockchain Governance. Proceedings of the 4th ACM Conference on Advances in Financial Technologies.

Kiayias, A., & Yung, M. (2015). Cryptographic Voting Protocols: A Systems Perspective. *Advances in Cryptology—CRYPTO 2015*, 312–332.

Kiely, Ray (2018), *The Neoliberal Paradox*. Northampton/MA: Edward Elgar.

Killmeier, M. A., & Chiba, N. (2010). Neo-nationalism seeks strength from the gods: Yasukuni Shrine, collective memory and the Japanese press. *Media, War & Conflict*, *3*(3), 334–354.

Komarčević, D. (2022). "Ruska invazija iskušava 'Otvoreni Balkan." *Radio Slobodna Evropa*. Prag. Retrieved from: <https://www.slobodnaevropa. org/a/rusija-invazija-ukrajina-test-otvoreni-balkan/31752336.html>.

Krekó, P., & Enyedi, Z. (2018). Explaining Eastern Europe: Orban's Laboratory of Illiberalism. Journal of Democracy, 29(3), 39–51.

Krimmer, R., Volkamer, M., Duenas-Cid, D., Kulyk, O., Ronne, P., Solvak, M., & Germann, M. (eds.) (2021). Electronic Voting. 6th International Joint Conference, E-Vote-ID, Virtual Event, October 5–8. Springer.

Kshetri, N., & Voas, J. (2018). Blockchain and Voting: Issues and Challenges Beyond Security. Computer, 51(10), 118–122.

Kuhler, Erol, Jean-Benoit Pilet. (2005). *Politics*: 25 (3), 153–164.

Kurti u Tirani predložio novi sporazum o slobodnoj trgovini, SEFTA umesto CEFTA, *Danas*. 10. jun 2021. Retrieved from: <https://www.danas.rs/vesti/ekonomija/kurti-u-tirani-predlozio-novi-sporazum-o-slobodnoj-trgovini-sefta-umesto-cefta/>, 23.04.2022.

Laclau, E. (2005). On populist reason (1. publ). Verso.

Lakićević D. A. (1999). "Roajomonski proces—jedna inicijativa za saradnju u Jugoistočnoj Evropi." *Međunarodni problemi*. LV (3–4): 401–413.

Lamer, M. (2005). Reaction & Resistance to Neo-liberalism in Zambia. *Review of African Political Economy, 32*(103), 29–45.

Lane, D. (2015). "Eurasian Integration as a Response to Neoliberal Globalization" In Lane, David ve Vsevolod Samokhvalov (eds.), *The Eurasian Project and Europe: Regional Discontinuities and Geopolitics* (pp. 3–22). New York: Palgrave Macmillan.

Larsson, A. O., & Skogerbø, E. (2018). Out with the old, in with the new? Perceptions of social (and other) media by local and regional Norwegian politicians. New Media & Society, 20(1), 219–236. <https://doi.org/10.1177/1461444816661549>

Laruelle, M. (2009). *In the Name of the Nation: Nationalism and Politics in Contemporary Russia*. Palgrave Macmillan.

Laver, M. (2004). Analyzing Structures of Party Preference in Electronic Voting Data. *Party Politics*, 10(5), 521–541.

Leonardis, M. de (2023). Introduction: NATO in Its Seventh Decade—A Reappraisal. In M. de Leonardis (ed.), *NATO in the Post-Cold War Era: Continuity and Transformation* (pp. 1–22). Cham: Palgrave Macmillan.

Lepskiy, M. & Lepska, N. (2023). The war in Ukraine and its challenge to NATO: Peacekeeping to peace engineering. *American Behavioral Scientist*, 67(3), 402–425.

Lessig, L. (1999). *Code and Other Laws of Cyberspace*. Basic Books.

Leston-Bandeira, C., Schwemmer, C., & Fernandes, J. M. (2016). Election Proximity and Representation Focus in Party-Constrained Environments. Party Politics, 24(2).

Levitsky, S., & Way, L. (2020). The New Competitive Authoritarianism. *Journal of Democracy*, 31(1), 51–65.

Lindner, R., Aichholzer, G., & Hennen, L. (2016). Electronic Democracy in Europe: Prospects and Challenges of E-Publics, E-Participation and E-Voting. Springer, NY.

Loader, B. D., & Mercea, D. (2012). Social Media and Democracy: Innovations in Participatory Politics. Routledge, London.

Loader, B. D., Vromen, A., & Xenos, M. A. (2014). *The networked young citizen: Social media, political participation, and civic engagement.* Routledge.

Lopandić, D., Kronja, J. (2010). *Regionalne inicijative i multilateralna saradnja na Balkanu.* Beograd: Evropski pokret u Srbiji. Friedrich Ebert Stiftung.

Lührmann, A., & Lindberg, S. I. (2019). A Third Wave of Autocratization Is Here: What Is New About It? *Democratization*, 26(7), 1095–1113.

Magnuson, W. (2020). *Blockchain Democracy: Technology, Law and the Rule of the Crowd.* Cambridge University Press.

Mann, R., & Fenton, S. (2017). *Nation, class and resentment: The politics of national identity in England, Scotland and Wales.* London: Springer.

McChesney, R. W. (2000a). Rich media, poor democracy: Communication politics in dubious times. Choice Reviews Online. <https://doi.org/10.5860/CHOICE.38-0115>

McChesney, R. W. (2000b). The Political Economy of Communication and the future of the Field. Media, Culture & Society SAGE Publication, 22, 109–116. <https://doi.org/10.1057/9781137480774_5>

McCormack, Conny B. (2016). *Why Use Electronic Voting?* Democracy Rebooted: The Future of Technology in Elections, Atlantic Council.

McCrone, D. (2002). *The Sociology of Nationalism: Tomorrow's Ancestors.* Londra: Routledge.

McEwen, N. (2018). Brexit and Scotland: Between two unions. *British Politics, 13*, 65–78.

McGann, A. J., & Kitschelt, H. (2005). The radical right in the Alps: evolution of support for the Swiss SVP and Austrian FPÖ. *Party Politics, 11*(2), pp. 147–171.

Mechkova, V., Lührmann, A., & Lindberg, S. I. (2017). How Much Democratic Backsliding? *Journal of Democracy*, 28(4), 162–169.

Meier, W. A., & Trappel, J. (2007). Power, Performance and Politics: Media Policy in Europe. Nomos.

Mendonca, M. R. F., Barreto, A. M. S., & Ziviani, A. (2021). Approximating Network Centrality Measures Using Node Embedding and Machine Learning. IEEE Transactions on Network Science and Engineering, 8(1), 220–230. <https://doi.org/10.1109/TNSE.2020.3035352>

Metz, F. L., & Neri, I. (2021). Localization and Universality of Eigenvectors in Directed Random Graphs. Physical Review Letters, 126(4), 040604. <https://doi.org/10.1103/PhysRevLett.126.040604>

Minkenberg, M., & Perrineau, P. (2007). The radical right in the European elections 2004. *International Political Science Review, 28*(1), 29–55.

Moffitt, B., & Tormey, S. (2014). Rethinking populism: Politics, mediatization and political style. Political Studies, 62(2), 381–397. <https://doi.org/10.1111/1467-9248.12032>

Morozov, E. (2011) The net delusion: The dark side of Internet freedom. PublicAffairs.

Mosco, V. (1996). Political economy of communication. <https://doi.org/10.4135/9781446279946>

Mounk, Y., & Kyle, J. (2018). What populists do to democracies. *The Atlantic, 26.*

Mudde, C. (1999). The single-issue party thesis: Extreme right parties and the immigration issue. *West European Politics, 22*(3), 182–197.

Mudde, C. (2004). The populist zeitgeist. *Government and opposition, 39*(4), pp. 541–563.

Mudde, C. (2004). The Populist Zeitgeist. In Government and Opposition (pp. 542–564). Blackwell publishing.

Mudde, C. (2015). Populist radical right parties in Europe today. In J. Abromeit, Y. Norman, G. Marotta, & B. Chesterton, *Transformations of Populism in Europe and the Americas: History and Recent Trends* (pp. 295–307). London: Bloomsbury.

Muharremi R. (2021). "The 'Washington Agreement' between Kosovo and Serbia," *American Society of International Law. Retrieved from:*

<https://www.asil.org/insights/volume/25/issue/4/washington-agreement-between-kosovo-and-serbia>. 14.04.2024.

Murphy, C., Johnson, M., & Bowler, S. (2007). Partisan Bias in Evaluating U. S. Elections during the HAVA Decade: A Natural Experiment. Presented at the Annual Meeting of the Western Political Science Association, Las Vegas, NV.

Naerland, T. U. (2016). Right-Wing Populism and Hip-Hop Music in Norway (9). 9, Article 9. <https://doi.org/10.18573/j.2016.10044>

Nakahara, J. (2021). Deconstructing Abe Shinzo's "Take Back Japan" Nationalism. *The Asia-Pacific Journal: Japan Focus, 19*(1), 1–13.

NATO (2017, August 8). Science & alliance: NATO's third dimension. Retrieved August 7, 2024, from <https://www.nato.int/nato_static_fl2014/assets/pdf/pdf_2017_08/20170808_Science-Alliance-NATO-Third-Dim.pdf>

NATO (2019, June 18). 60 years of Science for Peace and Security Program at NATO. Retrieved August 2, 2024, from <https://www.youtube.com/watch?v=iVWCUG-n5H8>

NATO (2020, December). Accelerating mine clearance in humanitarian demining operations. Retrieved July 18, 2024, from <https://www.nato.int/nato_static_fl2014/assets/pdf/2020/12/pdf/201204-sps-mine-clearance.pdf>

NATO (2021, November 4). A gender lens approach to military to civilian transition and reintegration for Ukraine Joint Forces Operation women combatants. Retrieved October 5, 2024, from <https://www.nato.int/nato_static_fl2014/assets/pdf/2021/11/pdf/2021-11-04-sps-arw-g5309-en.pdf>

NATO (2022, January 14). The safety and security of cultural heritage in zones of war or instability. Retrieved June 17, 2024, from <https://www.nato.int/cps/en/natohq/topics_190858.htm?>

NATO (2022, June 29). NATO 2022 Strategic Concept. Retrieved June 17, 2024, from <https://www.nato.int/nato_static_fl2014/assets/pdf/2022/6/pdf/290622-strategic-concept.pdf>

NATO (2022, October 14). Human security: Approach and guiding principles. Retrieved September 12, 2024, from <https://www.nato.int/cps/en/natohq/official_texts_208515.htm>

NATO (2023, April 17). Science for Peace and Security Program. Retrieved June 20, 2024, from <https://www.nato.int/cps/en/natohq/topics_85373.htm>

NATO (2024, April 11). Science for Peace and Security key priorities. Retrieved July 18, 2024, from <https://www.nato.int/cps/en/natohq/85291.htm>

NATO (2024, April 12). NATO releases first international strategy on biotechnology and human enhancement technologies. Retrieved August 2, 2024, from <https://www.nato.int/cps/en/natohq/news_222980.htm>

NATO (2024, April 19). NATO SPS Program Annual Report 2023. Retrieved July 18, 2024, from <https://www.nato.int/nato_static_fl2014/assets/pdf/2024/4/pdf/240419-SPS-AnnualReport2023.pdf>

NATO (2024, April 24). NATO and Gulf partners boost scientific cooperation on security implications of climate change. Retrieved July 17, 2024, from https://www.nato.int/cps/en/natohq/news_225024.htm

NATO (2024, August 8). Emerging and disruptive technologies. Retrieved August 22, 2024, from <https://www.nato.int/cps/en/natohq/topics_184303.htm>

NATO (2024, August 30). Human security agenda. Retrieved September 2, 2024, from <https://www.nato.int/nato_static_fl2014/assets/pdf/2024/8/pdf/240830-human-security-en.pdf>

NATO (2024, February 11). Inspired by nature—NATO supports scientists developing new technologies. Retrieved August 1, 2024, from <https://www.nato.int/cps/en/natohq/news_222582.htm>

NATO (2024, July 1). DIANA, NATO's defense innovation accelerator, launches new challenges. Retrieved July 10, 2024, from <https://www.nato.int/cps/en/natohq/news_227239.htm?selectedLocale=en>

NATO (2024, July 15). NATO's role in defense industry production. Retrieved July 20, 2024, from <https://www.nato.int/cps/en/natohq/topics_222589.htm>

NATO (2024, October 16). Fostering security-related scientific cooperation with Romania through NATO's SPS Program. Retrieved

October 20, 2024, from <https://www.nato.int/cps/en/natohq/news_229524.htm>

NATO (2024, October 22). NATO continues to strengthen 30 years of scientific cooperation with Bulgaria. Retrieved October 23, 2024, from <https://www.nato.int/cps/en/natohq/news_229986.htm>

NATO (2024, September 27). NATO's scientific cooperation with Azerbaijan. Retrieved October 1, 2024, from <https://www.nato.int/cps/en/natohq/news_229121.htm>

NATO (2024a, July 10). NATO releases revised AI strategy. Retrieved July 12, 2024, from <https://www.nato.int/cps/en/natohq/news_227234.htm>

NATO (2024b, July 10). Washington Summit declaration. Retrieved July 12, 2024, from <https://www.nato.int/cps/en/natohq/official_texts_227678.htm>

NATO CCOE (2023). The Israel-Hamas conflict: Civil-military implications. Retrieved July 12, 2024, from <https://www.cimic-coe.org/resources/isr-war-2023-cic-2.pdf>

NATO CCOE (2024). Case study: Ukraine. Retrieved September 2, 2024, from <https://www.cimic-coe.org/resources/fact-sheets/ccoe-case-study-ukraine-initial-study.pdf>

Neumann, I. B. (2013). *Russia and the idea of Europe: a study in identity and international relations.* London: Routledge.

Niemi, Richard G., Frederick G. Conrad, Michael W. Traugott, & Robert M. Sherman. (2008). Voters' Evaluations of Electronic Voting Systems: Results from a Usability Field Study. *American Politics Research*, 36(4), 580–611.

Nishiyama, H. (2023). Decolonial encounter with neo-nationalism: The politics of indigeneity and land rights struggles in Okinawa. *Transactions of the Institute of British Geographers*, 48(2), 290–303.

Nye, J. S. (1968). *International Regionalism: Readings.* Boston: Little Brown and Company.

Osmani i Pendarovski izrazili rezerve prema inicijativi "Otvoreni Balkan," Радио Слободна Европа, retrieved from; <https://www.

slobodnaevropa.org/a/otvoreni-balkan-osmani-penderovski/31610480.
html, 26.04.2024>.

Nye, J. S. (1971). *Peace in Parts: Integration and Conflict in Regional Organizations*. Boston: Little Brown and Company.

Østerud, Ø., & Selle, P. (2006). Power and Democracy in Norway: The Transformation of Norwegian Politics1. Scandinavian Political Studies, 29(1), 25–46. <https://doi.org/10.1111/j.1467-9477.2006.00140.x>

O'Toole, G. (2003). A new nationalism for a new era: The political ideology of Mexican neoliberalism. *Bulletin of Latin American Research*, 22(3), pp. 269–290.

Özdemir, Y. (2020). AKP's neoliberal populism and contradictions of new social policies in Turkey. Contemporary Politics, 26(3), 245–267. <https://doi.org/10.1080/13569775.2020.1720891>

Özmen, Y. P. (2022). Dijital çağda siyasal katılım: Toplumsal hareketler ve siyasi partiler. Mülkiye Dergisi, 46(3), p. 767–793.

Öztürk, E., & Zeybek, A. (2020). YouTube in Turkey's 2019 local elections: A case study of campaign communication. Journal of Communication Studies, 28(3), p. 65–80.

Palonen, E. (2018). Performing the nation: The Janus-faced populist foundations of illiberalism in Hungary. Journal of Contemporary European Studies, 26(3), 308–321. <https://doi.org/10.1080/14782804.201 8.1498776>

Paquin, S. (2007). Globalization, European Integration and the Rise of Neo-nationalism. *Nationalism and Ethnic Politics*, 8(1), 55–80.

Pasha, M. K. (2013). "The 'Bandung Impulse' and International Relations" In Seth, Sanjay (eds.), *Postcolonial Theory and International Relations: A Critical Introduction* (pp.144–165). New York: Routledge).

Pata, U. K., Destek, M. A., Manga, M. & Cengiz, O. (2023). Militarization of NATO countries sparks climate change? Investigating the moderating role of technological progress and financial development, Journal of Cleaner Production, 409, 1–13.

Penney, M., & Wakefield, B. (2009). Right Angles: Examining Accounts of Japanese Neo-nationalism. *Pacific Affairs, 81*(4), 537–555.

Pinar, E., & Gehring, A. (2023). "They Cannot Herd a Sheep" Populist Politics and Its Struggles for and Against Education in Turkey. Journal of Balkan and Near Eastern Studies, 25(3), 440–457. <https://doi.org/10.1080/19448953.2022.2143849>

Polanyi, K. (2007). *Büyük Dönüşüm: Çağımızın Sosyal ve Ekonomik Kökenleri.* İstanbul: İletişim. (Trans. Ayşe Buğra).

Popoveniuc, S., & Vora, P. L. (2010). Secure Electronic Voting—A Framework. *Cryptologia,* 34(3), 236–257.

Protesti u Tirani zbog dolaska Vučića, Radio Slobodna Evropa. Retrieved from: <https://www.slobodnaevropa.org/a/tirana-protestivu%C4%8Di%C4%87-otvoreni-balkan/31618133.html>, 22.8.2022.

Pugliese, G. (2015). The China Challenge, Abe Shinzo's Realism, and the Limits of Japanese Nationalism. *SAIS Review of International Affairs,* 35(2), pp. 45–55.

Putnam, R. D. (2000). *Bowling Alone: The Collapse and Revival of American Community.* Simon & Schuster.

Rheingold, H. (1993). *The Virtual Community: Homesteading on the Electronic Frontier.* Addison-Wesley.

Rodrik, D. (2021). Why does globalization fuel populism? Economics, culture, and the rise of right-wing populism. *Annual Review of Economics, 13*, pp. 133–170.

Rosén, F. (2017). *NATO and Cultural Property: Embracing New Challenges in the Era of Identity Wars,* Copenhagen: Nordic Center for Cultural Heritage & Armed Conflict.

Rosén, F. (2023). NATO and cultural property: A hybrid threat perspective. *PRISM, 10*(3), 45–58.

Saraph, A. (2011). An Agenda for Reform of the Election System in India. Economic and Political Weekly, 46(12), 19–24.

Sarmah, S. S. (2018). Understanding Blockchain Technology. Computer Science and Engineering, 8(2), 23–29.

Saylan, İ. (2011). *Sub-state nationalism within European integration process: a comparative study of Scottish, Basque and Kurdish cases.* Ankara: Bilkent Universitesi [Yayınlanmamış Doktora Tezi].

Schakel, A. H., & Romanova, V. (2022). Regional Assemblies and Executives, Regional Authority, and the Strategic Manipulation of

Regional Elections in Electoral Autocracies. *Regional and Federal Studies*, 32(4), 413–435.

Scheiring, G. (2018). Lessons from the Political Economy of Authoritarian Capitalism in Hungary. Transnational Institute WP, April 1–14.

Scheiring, G. (2020). Left behind in the Hungarian rustbelt: The cultural political economy of working-class neo-nationalism. *Sociology, 54*(6), pp. 1159–1177.

Schneider, R., & Bugarin, M. (2020). Electronic Voting and Public Spending: The Impact of De Facto Enfranchisement on Federal Budget Amendments in Brazil. *Journal of Applied Economics,* 23(1), 299–315.

Schneider, R., & Senters, K. N. (2018). Winners and Losers of the Ballot: Electronic vs. Traditional Paper Voting Systems in Brazil. Latin American Politics and Society, 60(2), 41–60.

Schwarzmantel, J. (2008). *Ideology and politics.* Sage.

Scott, J. (2017). Social Network Analysis (4th Edition). SAGE Publications. <https://uk.sagepub.com/en-gb/eur/social-network-analysis/book249668>

Scott, J., & Carrington, P. J. (2011). The SAGE Handbook of Social Network Analysis. SAGE.

Sedgwick, M. (2013). Something varied in the state of Denmark: Neo-nationalism, anti-Islamic activism, and street-level thuggery. *Politics, Religion & Ideology, 14*(2), pp. 208–233.

Seifman, R. (2024, July 16). NATO's human security mandate: Why it should include pandemic prevention, preparedness, and response. Retrieved October 5, 2024, from <https://impakter.com/natos-human-security-mandate-why-it-should-include-pandemic-prevention-preparedness-and-response/>

Selleslaghs, J., Luk V. L. (2020). "The Rise of Regions: Introduction to Regional Integration & Organizations" In Hosli, Madeleine O. ve Joren Selleslaghs (edst.). *The Changing Global Order: Challenges and Prospects* (pp. 147–162). Cham: Springer.

Shahandashti, S. F., & Hao, F. (2016). A Blockchain-Based Voting System. In *International Conference on Financial Cryptography and Data Security.* Springer.

Sjøvaag, H. (2012). Regulating commercial public service broadcasting: A case study of the marketization of Norwegian media policy. International Journal of Cultural Policy, 18(2), 223–237. <https://doi.org/10.1080/10286632.2011.573851>

Sjøvaag, H. (2014). The Principles of Regulation and the Assumption of Media Effects. Journal of Media Business Studies, 11(1), 5–20. <https://doi.org/10.1080/16522354.2014.11073573>

Sjøvaag, H., & Krumsvik, A. H. (2018). In Search of Journalism Funding: Scenarios for future media policy in Norway. Journalism Practice, 12(9), 1201–1219. <https://doi.org/10.1080/17512786.2017.1370972>

Slobodian, Q., (2023). *Crack-Up Capitalism: Market Radicals and the Dream of a World Without Democracy* (New York: Metropolitan Books).

Smith, A. D. (2004). *Milli Kimlik* (3. ed.). İstanbul: İletişim Yayınları.

[SRGSPSEE] Senior Review Group on the Stability Pact for South-Eastern Europe—Final Report. March 6, 2006. Retrieved from; <https://rai-see.org/wp-content/uploads/2016/02/Final-Report-of-the-SRG.pdf>.

Söderbaum, F. (2003). "Introduction: Theories of New Regionalism" In Söderbaum, Fredrik ve Timothy M. Shaw (eds.), *Theories of New Regionalism: a Palgrave Reader* (pp.1–21). New York: Palgrave Macmillan.

Söderbaum, F. (2016). "Early, Old, New, and Comparative Regionalism: The History and Scholarly Development of the Field" In Börzel, Tanja A. ve Thomas Risse (eds.), *The Oxford Handbook of Comparative Regionalism* (pp.16–40). Oxford: Oxford University Press.

Stein, R. M., Vonnahme, G., Byrne, M., & Wallach, D. (2008). Voting Technology, Election Administration, and Voter Performance. Election Law Journal, 7(2): 123–35.

Stier, S. (2015). Democracy, autocracy and the news: The impact of regime type on media freedom. Democratization, 22(7), 1273–1295. <https://doi.org/10.1080/13510347.2014.964643>

Storer, T., & Duncan, I. (2004). Polsterless Remote Electronic Voting. Journal of E-Government, 1(1), 75–103.

Sung, S. (2005). Japanese neo-nationalism and an idea of an East Asian community. *Inter-Asia Cultural Studies, 6*(4), 609–615.

Sunnercrantz, Liv. (2023, March 4). The impact of the Russia–Ukraine war on right-wing populism in Norway—ECPS. <https://www.populismstudies.org/the-impact-of-the-russia-ukraine-war-on-right-wing-populism-in-norway/>

Svolik, M. W. (2012). The politics of authoritarian rule. Cambridge University Press.

Swank, D., & Betz, H.-G. (2003). Globalization, the welfare state and right-wing populism in Western Europe. *Socio-Economic Review, 1*(2), 215–245.

Szebeni, Z., & Salojärvi, V. (2022). "Authentically" Maintaining Populism in Hungary—Visual Analysis of Prime Minister Viktor Orbán's Instagram. Mass Communication and Society, 25(6), 812–837. <https://doi.org/10.1080/15205436.2022.2111265>

Talani, L. S. (2016). "The Migration Crisis Before and After the Arab Spring: A Transnationalist Perspective" In Cafruny, A., Gonzalo Pozo Martin ve Leila Simona Talani, (eds.), *The Palgrave Handbook of Critical International Political Economy. (pp.209–238).* London: Palgrave Macmillan.

Teague, V., & Lewis, S. J. (2020). Voatz and the Risks of Blockchain Voting: A Security Analysis. *Proceedings of the 2020 IEEE Security and Privacy Workshops*, IEEE.

Thelwall, M. (2018). Social media analytics for YouTube comments: Potential and limitations. International Journal of Social Media and Interactive Learning Environments, 6(2), p. 108–123.

Theocharis, Y., & van Deth, J. W. (2018). *Political participation in a changing world: Conceptual and empirical challenges in the study of citizen engagement*. Routledge.

Thomas, P. (2020). Delegitimizing multicultural education: Populist politicians in Norway and the weaponizing of the autobiographical genre. European Politics and Society, 21(5), 520–534. <https://doi.org/10.1080/23745118.2019.1683984>

Tokaji, D. P. (2007). Leave It to the Lower Courts: On Judicial Intervention in Election Administration. *Ohio Law Journal*, 68, 1065–1095.

Tomaz, T., & Trappel, J. (2022). Democracy at stake: On the need of news media monitoring (pp. 11–31). Nordicom, University of Gothenburg. <https://urn.kb.se/resolve?urn=urn:nbn:se:norden:org:diva-12327>

Toth, T. (2020). Target the enemy: Explicit and implicit populism in the rhetoric of the Hungarian right. Journal of Contemporary European Studies, 28(3), 366–386. <https://doi.org/10.1080/1478280 4.2020.1757415>

Toumi, K., Aouadi, M., Cavalli, A. R., Mallouli, W., Allepuz, J. P., & Montfort, P. V. (2018). A Framework for Testing and Monitoring Security Policies: Application to an Electronic Voting System. Security in Computer Systems and Networks. The Computer Journal, 61(8).

Trosić S., Arnaudov, M. (2023). What are the Realistic Capabilities of the Berlin Process and the Open Balkans Initiative? *The Review of International Affairs.* Vol. LXXIV. No. 1187, Pp. 59–85.

UNDP (2022). 2022 Special Report: New threats to human security in the Anthropocene. Retrieved September 10, 2024, from <https://hdr.undp. org/system/files/documents/srhs2022.pdf>

Unfreedom Monitor · Global Voices. (2023). Global Voices. <https:// globalvoices.org/special/unfreedom-monitor/>

Vaagan, R. W. (2008). Media, market, state and politics in Norway. <https://oda.oslomet.no/oda-xmlui/handle/10642/471>

Van der Wende, M. (2020). Neo-nationalism and universities in Europe. *Research and Occasional Paper Series,* 7, pp. 1–16.

Van Der Wurff, R. (2008). Media Concentration and Democracy: Why Ownership Matters. Acta Politica, 43(1), 132–135. <https://doi. org/10.1057/palgrave.ap.5500214>

Vesilind, P. A. (2010). *Engineering Peace and Justice.* London: Springer-Verlag.

Vihma, A., Reischl, G., & Nonbo Andersen, A. (2021). A Climate Backlash: Comparing Populist Parties' Climate Policies in Denmark, Finland, and Sweden. The Journal of Environment & Development, 30(3), 219–239. <https://doi.org/10.1177/10704965211027748>

Vizcarrondo, T. (2013). Measuring Concentration of Media Ownership: 1976–2009. International Journal on Media Management, 15(3), 177–195. <https://doi.org/10.1080/14241277.2013.782499>

Vlahović, M. (2021). "'Otvoreni Balkan'—da se Vlasi ne sjete", *Portal Analitika*. Retrieved from: <https://www.portalanalitika.me/clanak/otvoreni-balkan-da-se-vlasi-ne-sjete>.

Vučić, Zaev i Rama potpisali deklaraciju o slobodnom protoku robe i ljudi., Radio Slobodna Evropa, retrieved from: <*https://www.slobodnaevropa.org/a/vucic-zaev-rama-novi-sad/30209132.html*>, 23.04.2024.

Walch, A. (2019). The Pathologies of Blockchain Governance. *European Business Organization Law Review*, 20(1), 19–37.

Walker, C. (1972). Nation-building or Nation-destroying? *World Politics*, 24(3), 319–355.

Wallmann, C., & Gerschberger, M. (2021). The association between network centrality measures and supply chain performance: The case of distribution networks. Procedia Computer Science, 180, 172–179. <https://doi.org/10.1016/j.procs.2021.01.153>

Wang, Z. (2021). From Crisis to Nationalism? *Chinese Political Science Review*, 6(1), pp. 20–39.

Wasserman, S., & Faust, K. (1994). Social Network Analysis: Methods and Applications. Cambridge University Press. <https://doi.org/10.1017/CBO9780511815478>

Wattenhofer, R. (2016). *The Science of the Blockchain*. Inverted Forest Publishing.

Weber, H., Poppy W. (2016). "The 'Bandung Spirit' and Solidarist Internationalism." *Australian Journal of International Affairs*. 70 (4), 391–406.

Weill, R. (2017) *Election Integrity: The Constitutionality of Transitioning to Electronic Voting in Comparative Terms*. Digital Democracy in a Globalized World, 142, 142–159 (Corien Prins et al. eds, Edward Elgar)

Wigell, M. (2008). Mapping "hybrid regimes": Regime types and concepts in comparative politics. Democratization, 15(2), 230–250. <https://doi.org/10.1080/13510340701846319>

Wigell, M. (2019). Democratic Deterrence. How To Dissuade Hybrid Interference. FIIA Working Paper, 110(September). <https://doi.org/10.1080/0163660X.2021.1893027>

Winichakul, T. (2008). Nationalism and the Radical Intelligentsia in Thailand. *Third World Quarterly, 29*(3), 575–591.

Winseck, D. (2008). The state of media ownership and media markets: Competition or concentration and why should we care? <https://doi.org/10.1111/J.1751-9020.2007.00061.X>

Winseck, D. (2022). Growth and Upheaval in the Network Media Economy, 1984–2021. Carleton University.

Wu, G. (2008). From Post-imperial to Late Communist Nationalism: Historical Change in Chinese Nationalism from May Fourth to the 1990s. *Third World Quarterly, 28*(3), 467–482.

Yanatma, S. (2021). Advertising and Media Capture in Turkey: How Does the State Emerge as the Largest Advertiser with the Rise of Competitive Authoritarianism? The International Journal of Press/Politics, 26(4), 797–821. <https://doi.org/10.1177/19401612211018610>

Yilmaz, I. (2023). The Nexus of Digital Authoritarianism and Religious Populism. Religions, 14(6), Article 6. <https://doi.org/10.3390/rel14060747>

Yilmaz, I., & Erturk, O. F. (2021). Populism, violence and authoritarian stability: Necropolitics in Turkey. Third World Quarterly, 42(7), 1524–1543. <https://doi.org/10.1080/01436597.2021.1896965>

Yilmaz, I., Shipoli, E., & Demir, M. (2021). Authoritarian resilience through securitization: An Islamist populist party's co-optation of a secularist far-right party. Democratization, 28(6), 1115–1132. <https://doi.org/10.1080/13510347.2021.1891412>

Zeng, G., He, M., Yiu, S. M., & Huang, Z. (2022). A Self-Tallying Electronic Voting Based on Blockchain. *Security in Computer Systems and Networks. The Computer Journal*, 65(12).

Zhou, S. (2022). The origins, characteristics and trends of neo-nationalism in the 21st century. *International Journal of Anthropology and Ethnology, 6*(1), 1–20.

Zuev, D. (2010). The movement against illegal immigration: analysis of the central node in the Russian extreme-right movement. *Nations and Nationalism, 16*(2), pp. 261–284.

Notes on Contributors

Esra Albayrakoğlu
Prof., Bahcesehir University, Faculty of Economics, Administrative and Social Sciences, Political Science and International Relations

Selcen Altınbaş-Umut
Asst. Prof., Istanbul Nişantaşı University, Political Science and Public Administration

F. Gamze Çakmak
Dr. Trakya University, Faculty of Applied Sciences, International Relations

Çiğdem Çelik
Dr. / Political Scientist

Sinem Eray
Dr. / Political Scientist

Günce Sabah Eryılmaz
Asst. Prof., Bahçeşehir University, Political Science and International Relations

Arda Can Kumbaracıbaşı
Assoc. Prof., Göttingen University

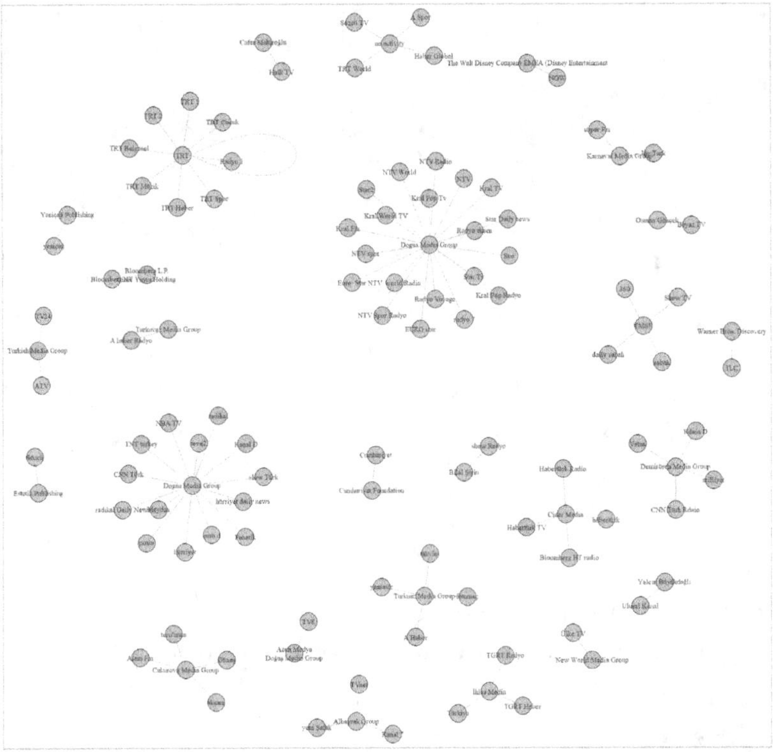

Figure 3.1. Turkey Media Network 2010

https://supplementaryresources.blob.core.windows.net/4333499-eray/Figure%203.1a.png

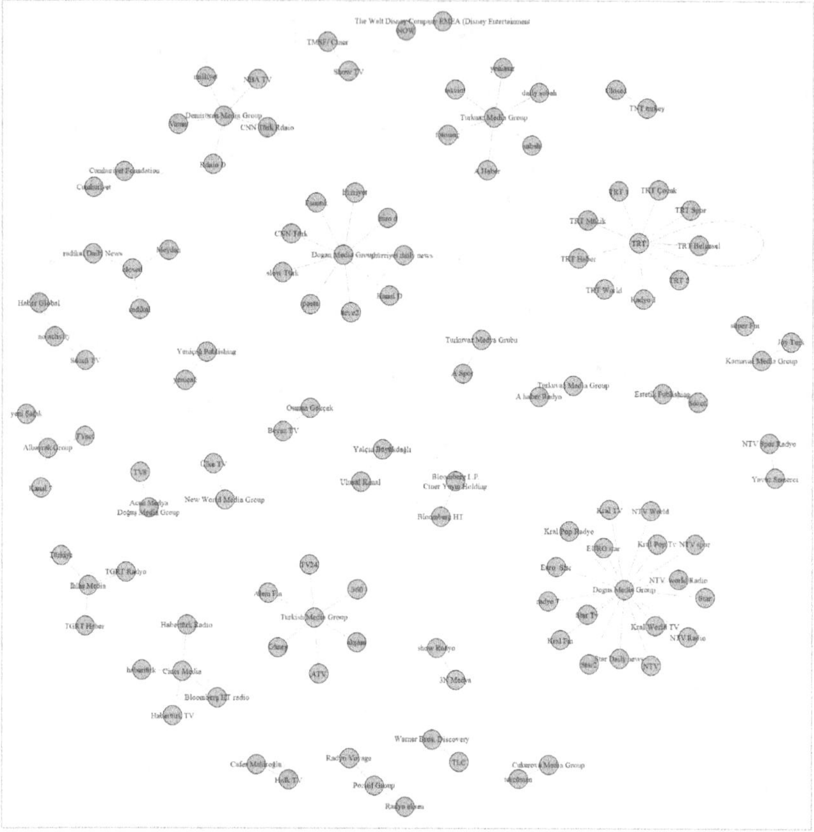

Figure 3.1. Turkey Media Network 2016

https://supplementaryresources.blob.core.windows.net/4333499-eray/Figure%203.1b.png

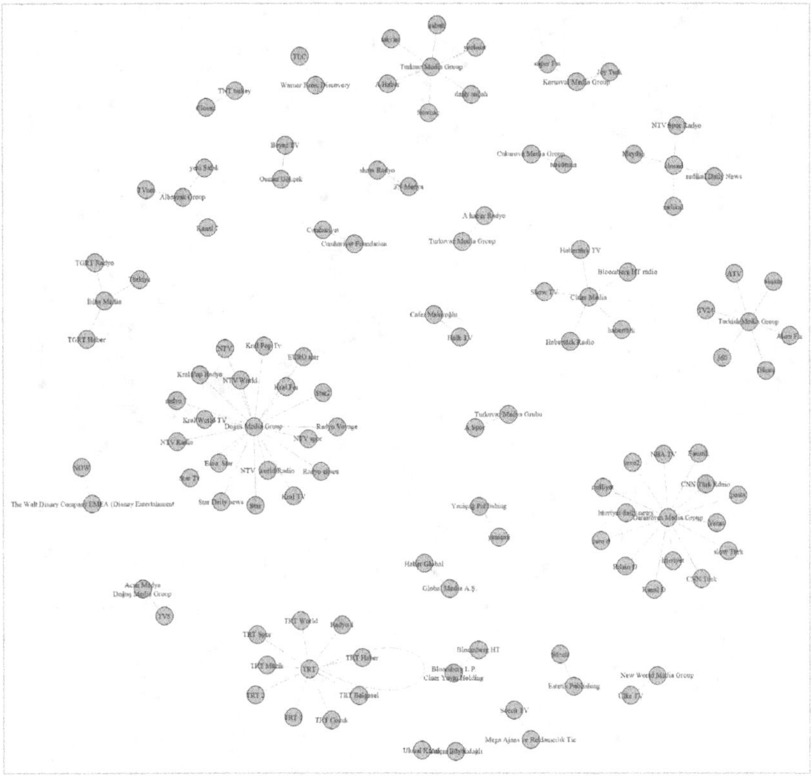

Figure 3.1. Turkey Media Network 2022

https://supplementaryresources.blob.core.windows.net/4333499-eray/Figure%203.1c.png

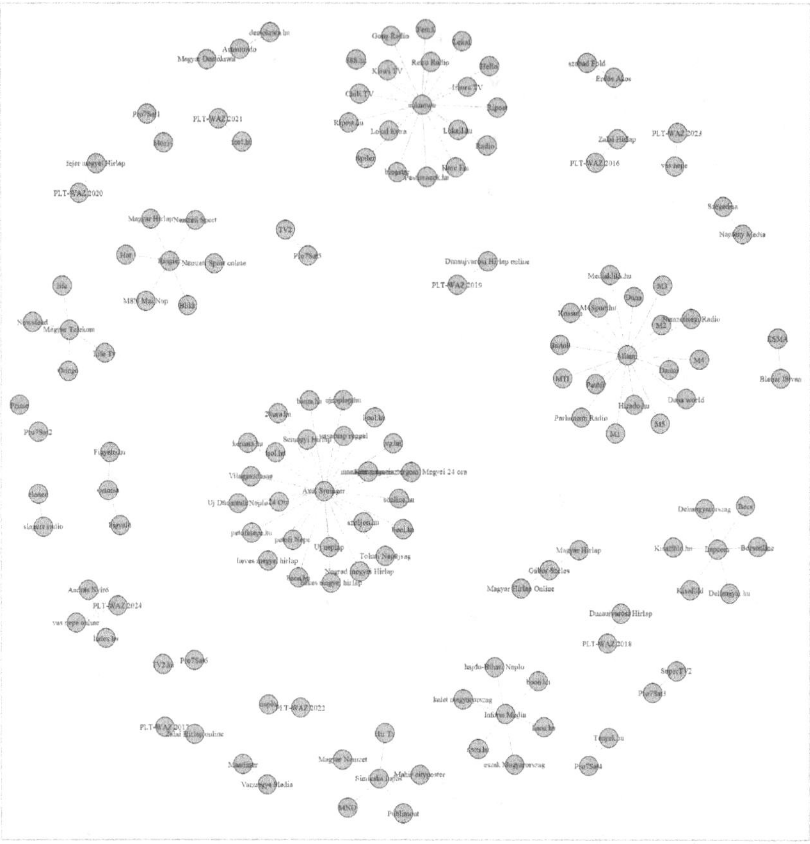

Figure 3.2. Hungary Media Network 2010

https://supplementaryresources.blob.core.windows.net/4333499-eray/Figure%203.2a.png

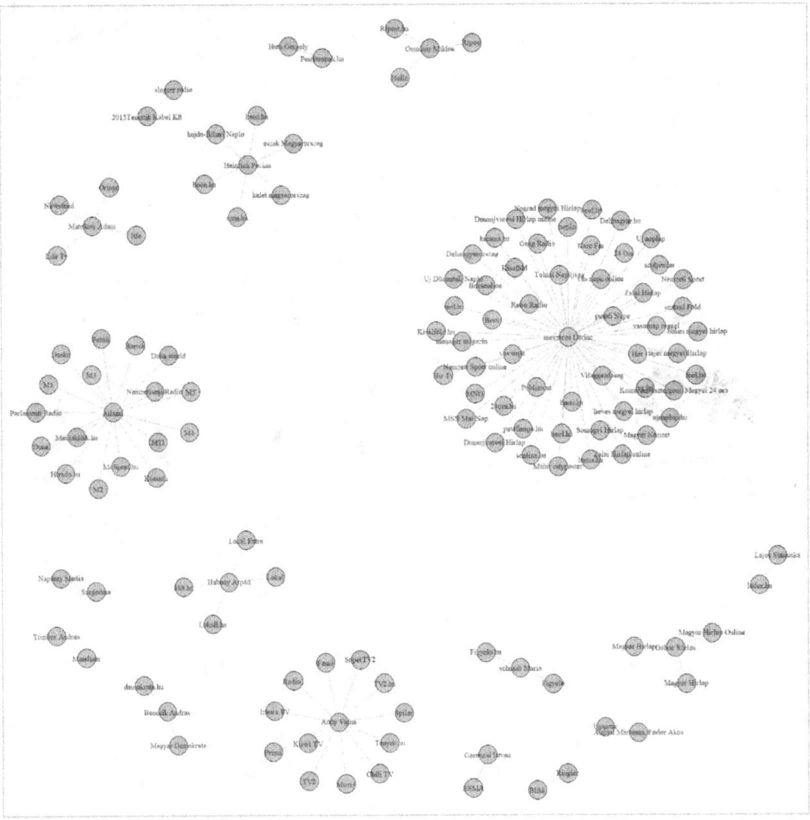

Figure 3.2. Hungary Media Network 2016

https://supplementaryresources.blob.core.windows.net/4333499-eray/Figure%203.2b.png

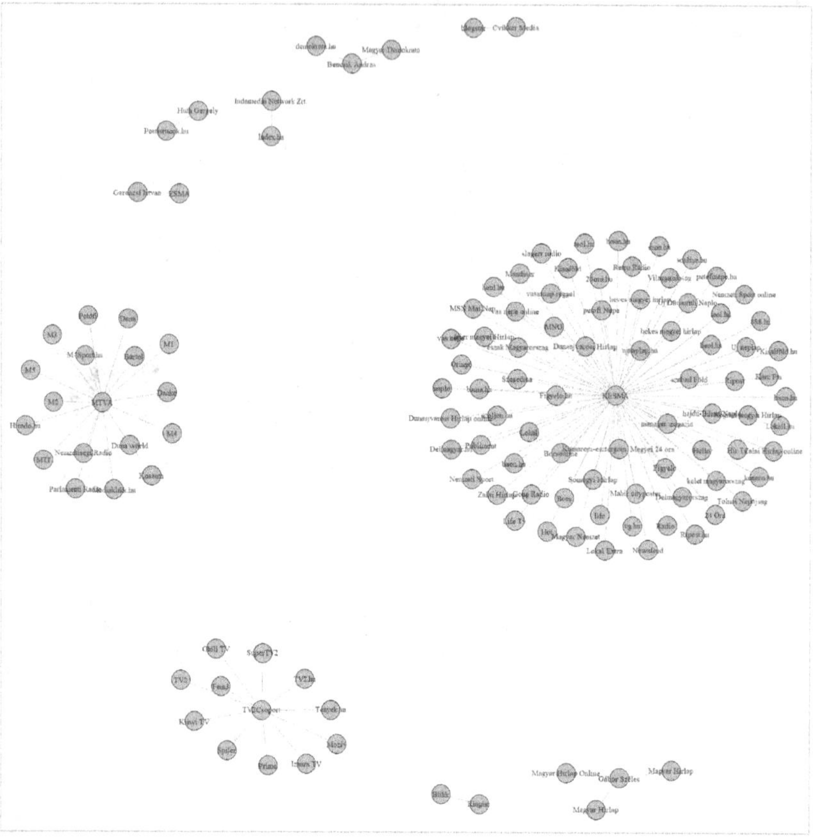

Figure 3.2. Hungary Media Network 2022

https://supplementaryresources.blob.core.windows.net/4333499-eray/Figure%203.2c.png

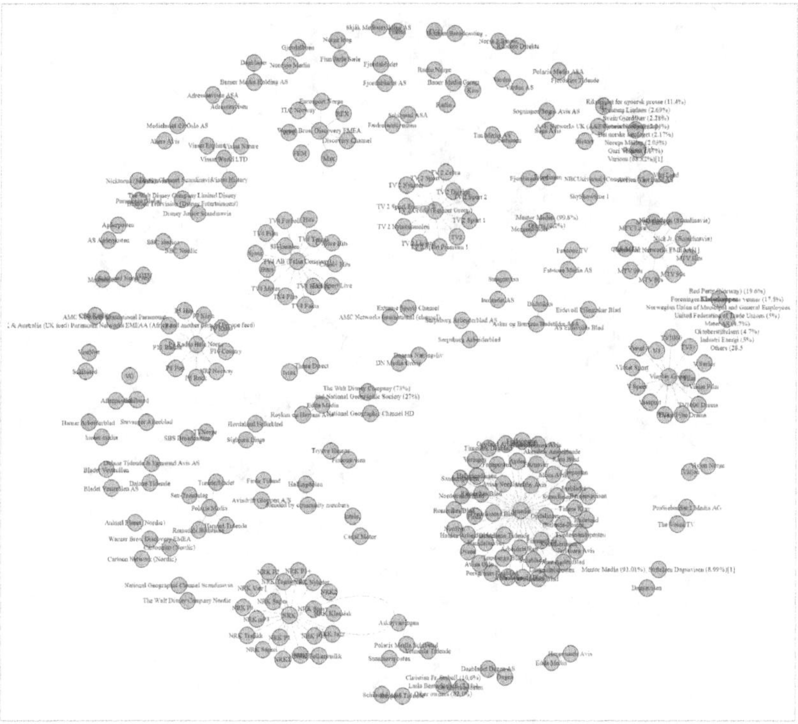

Figure 3.3. Norway Media Network 2010

https://supplementaryresources.blob.core.windows.net/4333499-eray/Figure%203.3a.png

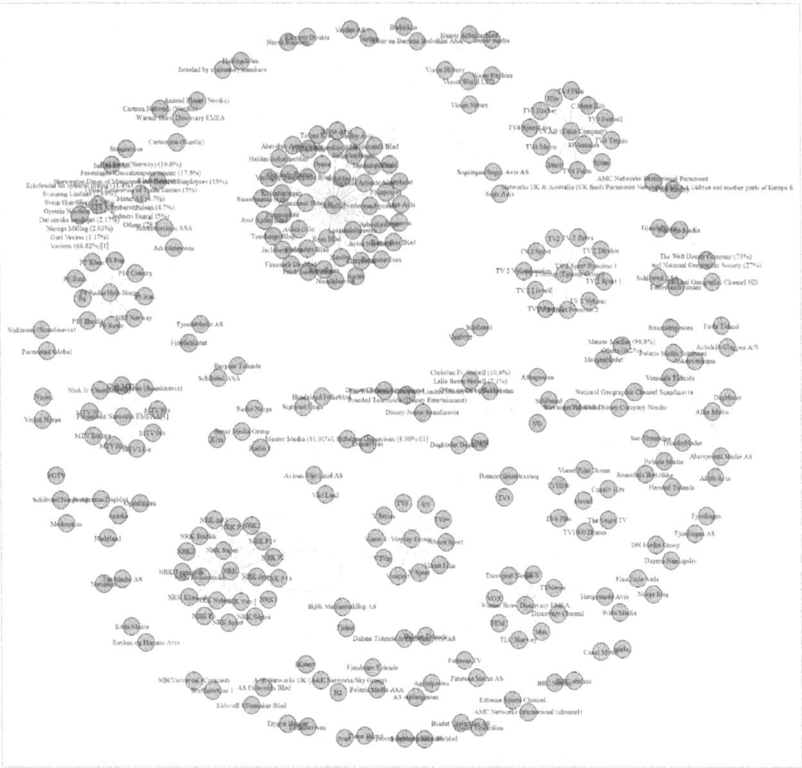

Figure 3.3. Norway Media Network 2016

https://supplementaryresources.blob.core.windows.net/4333499-eray/Figure%203.3b.png

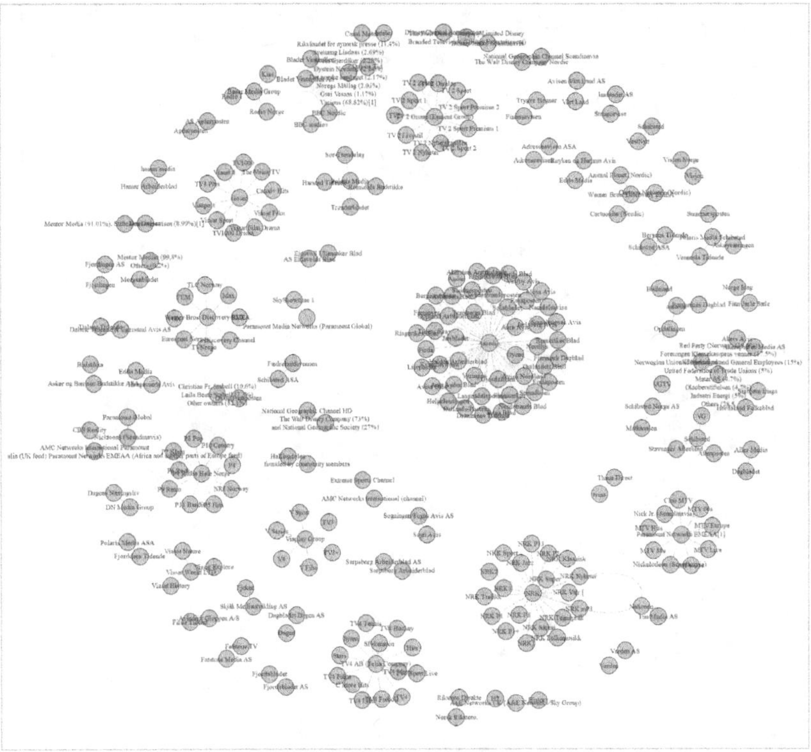

Figure 3.3. Norway Media Network 2022

https://supplementaryresources.blob.core.windows.net/4333499-eray/Figure%203.3c.png